The College Strategy Guide

The College Strategy Guide

College Is Easy

Gabe Barrett

Art by Jeff Lawrence

WESTBOW
P R E S S
A DIVISION OF THOMAS NELSON

WestBow Press books may be ordered through booksellers or by contacting:

WestBow Press
A Division of Thomas Nelson
1663 Liberty Drive
Bloomington, IN 47403
www.westbowpress.com
1-(866) 928-1240

Because of the dynamic nature of the Internet, any Web addresses or links contained in this book may have changed since publication and may no longer be valid. The views expressed in this work are solely those of the author and do not necessarily reflect the views of the publisher, and the publisher hereby disclaims any responsibility for them.

ISBN: 978-1-4497-0432-2 (sc)
ISBN: 978-1-4497-0431-5 (e)

Library of Congress Control Number: 2010934058

Printed in the United States of America

WestBow Press rev. date: 08/04/2010

This book is dedicated to
all the people who made the last five years
awesome. I've got more stories to tell
than I know what to do with.

Contents

ACKNOWLEDGMENTS

A big thank you goes out to Sandra and Len. Brian, I appreciate all the opinions I borrowed that I've yet to return. I thank Coach Yox for always making me finish through the line, and I thank Cassie for putting up with me when she doesn't have to. I can't leave out Chette, Jason, and Jennifer. And a very special thanks goes to Nathan and Lindsay.

Foreword

College is not your friend. It's an obstacle. And to accomplish your goals in life, it's something you have to defeat. If you ever want to see that fat paycheck, you have to finish. You have to walk across that stage and receive that piece of paper, because that's why you're here. The parties and intramurals are awesome. Staying up until 6:00 AM watching movies is a blast. Spending as much time as possible with friends you might only see once or twice after you leave is a must. But you *have* to graduate. This is one of the few instances in life in which the destination is just as important as the journey. Graduation takes the rest of life's journeys to a whole new level.

But, at the same time, it can't be just about class and what grade you earned on the chemistry final. When it's all said and done, you won't even remember those things. However, you will remember the Waffle House at 4:00 AM and the concert you went to instead of writing that term paper. *The key is balance.* To succeed in all this, you have to manage your time and energy in a way that is fun but also gets the job done. College is just a really expensive field trip if you don't come away with a diploma; but it's a mind-numbing chore if all you do is study and revise papers.

You have to find the median, and to accomplish that you need a strategy.

I wrote this book because I couldn't find anything out there that really worked. Every other book I found had been written by some forty-year-old who hadn't been in college since the nineties. I think times have changed a little bit, so I set out to write something relevant—a book with as little useless information as possible. You might think some (or even all) of it is common sense; if that's the case, then you're well in front of the pack. But if you're like me, then you have all the big stuff covered and won't figure out the details until three years in. I don't want that to happen to you like it did me; I want you to know as much as possible up front.

This book will give you everything you need to know to create a strategy that will conquer college. Don't just get by. Dominate the thing. It takes work, but it's not nearly as hard as people make it. Let me be the first to tell you that college can be one of the easiest things you'll ever do. All you need is the right information, the right attitude, and to understand the system. I'm not saying you won't have to put forth a great deal of effort or sacrifice some of your time, but just think: at what other point in life will you have this little responsibility, this few bills, and this many opportunities to do whatever you want? I mean where else is twelve hours considered full time?

1: GENERAL

A lot of crap about college doesn't fit into neat little categories, so it wound up here.

College Isn't Where You Find Yourself;
It's Where You Create Yourself

If you want to find yourself, move to Nepal. If you want to create yourself, go to college. High school is over. Your hometown is now a vacation spot. And whoever you used to be has no bearing on who you can be. No one knows what you looked like in seventh grade. No one knows who your parents are. No one knows any of those embarrassing stories you've been hoping people would forget. No one has any previous knowledge of you at all; so who you are *now* is who you are. It's time to create yourself. It's time to figure out what you like and whom you like. It's time to be what *you* want. I realize how cheesy that may sound. You may have even rolled your eyes at the idea. But here's the deal: a few years from now, you're going to be a completely different person whether you like it or not. Experiences, relationships, and how you spend your time are going to drastically alter who you are. The question is whether you'll see it and appreciate it as it happens or if you'll wake up one day and wonder what happened to you.

The better you understand the decisions you're making and how they affect you, the more you'll enjoy college as it happens and the less likely you are to have a moment when you wonder *Where did all the time go? Why didn't I slow down to appreciate it?* This is quite possibly the hardest thing about college, which is why I put it first in this book. If you can master this, if you can train yourself to revel in experiences as they occur, then you stand a good chance of dominating college. I'm not saying you'll leave with a 4.0, but college is about a lot more than grades.

Don't Go Home

When the weekend rolls around, it's perfectly normal to miss home and want to go back to how things were. It's also normal to grow up and move on with your life. So don't go home for a while. Wait at least a month. Leaving too soon means missing all the events colleges and dorms plan early in the semester to help everyone get to know each other. It also means missing all the free food. I know your mother cooks better than the cafeteria. I realize your roommate probably smells funny. But going home won't fix those problems. All the issues you leave will be waiting for you when you get back on Sunday night. And the more you go home, the more you don't want to come back to school, which also happens to make you much less likely to graduate. I'm not saying never look back or forget where you came from. Just don't go back until you're settled into your new home. Don't leave until you've adjusted to your new surroundings. Once you're comfortable, by all means, go back home. Take your dirty laundry. It'll save you quarters and make your folks feel wanted.

Good Things Come to Those Who Wait

College doesn't. Go sign up for things. Seek out opportunities. Want to work on the campus newspaper? Go talk to the people over at the campus newspaper. Want to be on the rugby team? Find their Web site and see who's in charge of it. Don't just assume a club, team, or job is going to come find you. You have to do the work yourself. No one's going to pass a sign-up sheet around in first period to see if you're interested. Remember, this is not high school. During the first few weeks of class, you'll probably see signs and flyers around campus detailing club meetings, team tryouts, and where to find job applications. Unsure about what you want to do? Go to informational meetings. Talk to people who are already in the groups you are interested in joining. You're not obligated to do anything, and it won't cost you a dime. College is full of free time, and these extracurricular activities will help make that time both fun and productive.

Read Bulletin Boards

They're full of information about job openings, apartment rentals, free puppies, fund-raisers, charities, guest speakers, concerts, contests, scholarships, and upcoming university events. (And those are just what I'm finding on the board I'm looking at right now.) You never know when an opportunity that is perfect for you will be posted. They change week to week, so check them out often.

Read Everything

The university often sends e-mails and letters containing important information on deadlines, requirements, and specific dates. Don't get messed up because you never checked your e-mail or just assumed those letters were garbage. It only takes a few seconds to figure out whether the info is important or not, and missing, say, a financial aid form deadline can cost you thousands of dollars. They're going to send you a lot of crap, and a lot of it really is junk mail, but don't let the one piece of pertinent news go unread because you were too lazy to open it.

Go to the Welcome Week Events

I know they're a little cheesy. I know they can be dull and seem like a waste of time. But they are absolutely packed with information, and more importantly, they're full of people who need to make friends as badly as you do. These events provide insights on subjects ranging from how to navigate the library's Web site to how to sign up for classes to how to stay safe on campus at night. In a lot of cases, these programs are the only opportunity for you to learn certain things about campus life. Don't be left in the dark because you were too cool to go. Plus, a lot of other people are going to be there, which makes it a prime time to meet new people and enhance your social network. Knowing a lot of people is a good thing. You don't have to be everybody's BFF, but the relationships you make in the first couple of weeks of class lay the foundation for the next four to seven years. So go play those stupid icebreaker games. You're likely to meet some pretty interesting people. (Oh, and these events usually have free food.)

The Mail Box Can Make Your Day (or Crush Your Soul)
Never before has opening up a small metal box had so much to do with your mood. Even if it's nothing but junk mail, it feels good to get something with your name on it that's not addressed to your parents' house. Wanna make someone's day? Put a note in his box complimenting his new mouthwash. Wanna ruin someone's day? Put a note in her box that says, "There's something in your teeth." Be prepared for disappointment; it may take a while for credit card companies to find you. Also, care packages from home are basically equal to Christmas. If you get a letter from home that doesn't have money in it, you should do something shocking: send a letter back that doesn't even ask for any. (Unless you're out of ramen. Then you should request a dollar to buy groceries for the week.)

Double-Check the Alarm

Don't be late or miss class because you forgot to change the PM to AM on your alarm clock. Your mom's not here to nag and pull the covers off you, so get in the habit of checking twice to make sure your wake-up time is right. It takes two seconds. Don't let something so simple ruin your day.

Road-Trip Frequently

Some of the greatest experiences of your life will happen on road trips with friends. (They've even been known to happen with people you barely know.) Just get in the car and drive. Go anywhere. Stop and do anything. Just go. Gas too expensive? Not if you split the cost between five people. Eat gas station food. Visit far off lands like the next county over. It's amazing what kinds of places you find when you look. Some great restaurants and putt-putt courses are out in the middle of nowhere. Seek them out. Make a few really great stories.

Self-Discipline

Here's the thing about self-discipline: ***the more you have, the faster you graduate.*** The better you are at making yourself go to class, studying when you don't want to, and grinding out those last three pages of a paper, the quicker you'll get your diploma and start getting paid. Failing classes because of laziness and lack of effort is pretty much inexcusable. In all honesty, college isn't that hard. Go to class. Do what the professor asks. Turn your work in on time. Study for the tests. And put forth the effort. Self-discipline governs all of these things. It's going to be a struggle, but you have to force yourself to do what it takes to get out of here. Don't end up being a fifth-year super senior with an ugly GPA.

It costs you time, money, and probably even self-esteem. So take responsibility for your actions, and force yourself to work hard. You'll graduate a lot faster.

Make To-Do Lists
It gets hard to keep track of everything you need to get done. From writing a ten-page paper to taking out the trash, college is full of tasks that can be easily forgotten. Solution? To-do lists. Write them on note cards or put them on napkins—just about anything you can fold up and put in your pocket. You will be amazed at how much more organized and efficient you can become when you have everything you need to do written down. And be sure to feel really good about yourself when you cross things off. Keeping lists is also nice because you can track your productivity. (To feel especially productive, make the list as specific as possible. Put items like "eat dinner" and "watch football game" right under "study" and "write paper." If you write it down, it feels more planned, which makes you feel more productive.)

Watch As Many Movies As You Can
After college, the time you'll have to watch movies will be decimated. So watch as many as you can now. Quality doesn't matter. Sometimes the worse the movie is, the better. Making fun of crappy dialogue is an art form. And, if you really want to spice things up, find the RiffTrax and play them with the movie. DVD delivery services like Netflix are also a good way to go. For a few bucks per month, you can watch a ton of movies and never worry about late fees. It's just made for college. (And for the record, *Indiana Jones 4* doesn't exist. The whole thing's a lie.)

Read As Many Books As You Can
Much like with movies, once you get out of here, your time to read evaporates. Take advantage of free time and expand your mind. Reading is a great way to relax before you go to sleep, books can be excessively entertaining, and reading will even make you a better student. Reading a lot tends to make you a better and faster reader, which comes in handy when you're stuck in World Lit. 2. Oh, books have also been known to change people's lives. And I'm not even talking about ones written by Dr. Phil. I mean books you'll likely find at the library. You're paying for the thing, so you might as well use it. Plus, it's rumored to have good books on every subject.

Save All Receipts, Forms, and Paperwork
Universities have been known to ask people to pay tuition twice, so save copies of all financial paperwork. With thousands of students to keep track of, glitches happen and information gets lost. Don't just assume the lady at the front desk will remember you paying your bill; keep the receipt. It's a really good idea to get a file organizer and label it well. Put copies of every transaction between you and the university in it, and keep it in a safe place. You never know when the computer will decide it's your turn to have your data corrupted. Avoid the hassle by keeping good records.

The Campus Will Change in Appearance
Campuses look completely different during orientation, homecoming, and family weekend. Universities realize who pays the bills. Don't be surprised when new flowers appear around the student center and fresh paint shows up in the cafeteria. Don't worry, in two weeks time all the flowers will have been stepped on and killed and the new paint will have philosophical writings as

profound as "Steve wuz here." Just enjoy the fact that your campus at least has the potential to look really nice.

Spring Break
You don't have to spend your spring break drunk on a beach. I realize it provides a rare relief from the monotony of studying and the other general rigors of college life, but it's also a prime opportunity to do something for someone other than yourself. There are plenty of groups that go to plenty of places on spring break to help people in need, and I'm sure they would love to have you join them. College can be the most selfish time of your life, which is understandable. You're trying to figure out what *you* want to do, where *you* want to live, and whom *you* want to be with. College is designed to be somewhat selfish. But don't let the whole thing be about you. Go do something for someone else. You'll meet some really great people and visit some unbelievable places. You'll even make the world a better place to live in, which, in the grand scheme of things, kicks the crap out of getting sunburned and finding sand stuck in your butt. (People have also been known to discover their true passions in life on these trips. It's funny how helping others can be the best way to learn about ourselves.)

Wrestling Is Back in Style
You probably haven't seen it in a while and probably have no idea what's going on, but that has nothing to do with how ridiculously amazing professional wrestling is. The storylines make soap operas wince, but who cares about the stories? You watch wrestling to see 270-pound men do back flips and land on other 270-pound men. Yes, the matches are rigged, and outcomes have been decided in

advance, but nothing about pro wrestling is fake. The collisions are real, chair shots to the face really do hurt, and the injuries can be devastating. It's great to watch in order to get your violence fix when football is out of season. The fanfare is incredible, and you have to admit that standing on a turnbuckle with seventy thousand people chanting your name would be pretty freaking awesome. (It's the whole working 350 days per year and utterly destroying your body that keeps it from being the perfect career.) And on a Monday night, when there's nothing else to do, watching wrestling can give you and your friends a good alternative to studying or getting wasted.

Résumé Building

The first rule of college is to graduate. The second is to enjoy the time you're there. Don't let college become one big résumé builder. I know you want to get a great job and drive a nice car and that a stellar résumé is helpful. But doing something for the sole reason that it looks good on your résumé is a bunch of garbage. If you're going to join a club or organization, you should *want* to be part of it. You should take pride in it and hopefully actually enjoy it. Employers don't want to know what you were involved in. They want to know what *you **did*** in what you were involved in. It's way better to be the president of some unknown, unpopular club than to be just some random member of a prestigious organization. Employers want to see if you're truly committed to something you enjoy or if you're just showing up to meetings because they'll void your membership if you don't. So if you're going to do something, do it wholeheartedly. That will take you a lot farther than doing something just because it looks good. (When typing the word résumé, to avoid having to add the accent marks manually, type the word resom. Most spellcheckers will ask if you want to change it to résumé.)

Stock Up on Duct Tape

If you can't fix it with duct tape, then it's probably not worth fixing. This little gray invention can solve problems from broken car fenders to leaky pipes. Stock up on it. It's cheap, and its uses are nearly infinite. Keep some in your car, your room, and even your book bag. You'll never know when you'll need it, but trust me, you will need it.

Parking

Parking on campus probably sucks. It's just one of those things you have to get used to. You'll probably hear a lot of people complain that there aren't enough spots. I assure you that there are plenty of spots; just very few of them are convenient. You have to weigh the options: Drive around in circles waiting for someone to leave and risk wasting an hour of your life? Or park really far away and walk to wherever you're going? I warn you not to choose the third option: park illegally. Many a campus salary is paid through parking tickets, and trust me, *they will get you.* A group of people is paid to seek out violators and punish them accordingly. That's their job; it's all they do. So don't park in that handicapped spot and think, *it'll only be a second.* And never turn your flashers on, as that just leads campus security right to you. The yellow lights are like a beacon guiding a ticket to your windshield. If you have to run a quick errand and know there won't be a spot, take a friend who can either sit in the car and move it if someone starts to write a ticket or circle the parking lot until you get back. (Accrue enough tickets, and they might not let you park on campus anymore.)

Alone Time Is a Luxury

College can be kinda crowded. Classes can have hundreds of people. House parties can be packed wall-to-wall. And the fast-food restaurant across from campus can have lines that stretch out the door. However, real life can be very, very lonely. So enjoy the fact that you can always find someone who will go out with you for food at 4:00 AM. With that said, it's important to find time to be by yourself. Don't take *too* much time for yourself, but find enough to keep from losing your mind. College can be overwhelming, and being alone can help you relax. But as soon as you feel better, go do something. You've got the rest of your life to be alone; college is about getting to know as many people as possible.

Day In, Day Out

College is going to have you questioning everything. Your beliefs and morals will come under scrutiny often. Ideas you've had your whole life will be ripped apart and handed back for you to figure out. Professors and students from widely differing backgrounds and with completely different points of view will be talking to you on a daily basis. They'll challenge you with new thoughts and opinions about every subject imaginable. The good news is that your thoughts and opinions will challenge them just as much. Embrace the questioning of your beliefs and ideas. Use this as a time to really figure life out. You're not going to have some deep philosophical discussion every day (unless you're a philosophy major), but they will happen from time to time. Use them as opportunities to learn and develop your own ideas. Your parents aren't here to tell you what to do anymore; now you have to figure it out for yourself. So, go figure it out.

Bathrooms

Map Them Out

Your campus is full of some very gross bathrooms. It's important to find out where the clean ones are before a drastic time of need. It's usually best to go where the fewest people are. Bathrooms you find in the random, barely used parts of buildings, around professors' offices, and in low traffic areas of new buildings are probably your best bets. If you can just find one really clean and hopefully quiet bathroom that is centrally located near all of your classes and activities, your college experience will be greatly enhanced. It may seem like a small, unimportant detail, but when you're about to poop your pants, it's nice to know where to find a seat without pee all over it. I mean, we're talking about the most private thing a person does on a daily basis here. It's nice to be able to relax in a clean environment that doesn't have people constantly wandering through it. The only downside to using these "off the beaten path" restrooms is that the stall wall literature will often be a little lacking. This is a small price to pay, I assure you.

Flush the Toilet

Flushing the toilet is really not a hard concept. Yet, you will find many a toilet around campus that still holds the gift one of your classmates decided to leave behind. Be a little considerate of others. If you don't want to touch the handle, then kick it with your foot.

Motion Sensors

A lot of toilets flush using motion sensors, which is great because you no longer have to stumble across what someone else left behind. However, the sensor can be a real hassle when you're trying to use the bathroom. If you move at all, the toilet tends to notice it and will often flush prematurely. (And a wet butt is no fun for anybody.) To avoid this, take a small stretch of toilet paper and drape it over the sensor before you sit down. Just be sure to remove it when you're done. (Oh, and fun fact for the day: corn is nature's bookmark.)

Mirrors

If you've just gotten out of the shower and your mirror is all fogged up, you can use a hair dryer to clear it off. It only takes a few seconds, and it won't leave any streaks like wiping it off with a towel will.

For Guys

In a guy's bathroom, it's a good rule of thumb to always leave the toilet seat up when you get done using it. This will ensure the idiot up the hall won't come in drunk at 3:00 AM and pee all over everything just so you can sit in it the next day. If girls use the bathroom at all, then this isn't a good idea, but as long as it's dudes only, put the seat down only when you need it.

2: HEALTH

Y ou're pretty much nothing without your health. All the studying in the world won't help you if your body is too tired, sick, or stressed out to remember the information. And you're much less likely to go to class when you feel like crap. *You have to take care of your body.* Not doing so will kill your grades, hurt your relationships, and can even lead to moving back home.

Stretch

Stretch before you leave in the morning and before you go to sleep at night. It only takes a few minutes and can make you feel a lot better. In the morning, stretching will loosen you up and get your body ready for the day. It'll get your blood flowing and help wake you up. At night, stretching can help relieve the stress your body endured during the day. It will reduce the knots that have taken hold in your trigger points and will make your body just feel better. Stretching is extremely important if you exercise. Playing intramurals, running, and working out will break down muscles and cause them to tighten. Stretching will minimize soreness and promote healing. Also, the longer a muscle is, the stronger it can be, and the more flexible you are, the less prone to injury you are. Stretching is an often-overlooked activity that can make a huge difference in how your body feels.

Wash Your Hands

This can be the single most important way to avoid sickness. I realize how cliché it is. I know you've been hearing it since you've had hands. But that's probably because it's really important. You're sharing space with a lot of people. You're breathing the same air and touching the same handrails. You don't want all of those people touching your food, too. So wash your hands—especially during flu season and after you work out. A lot of people use that same exercise equipment. Carrying hand sanitizer in your bag is also a good idea.

Hydrate

Dehydration will wreck your immune system, hurt your memory, and impair your judgment. I'm not saying you have to drink a gallon of water per day or anything, but not drinking enough can seriously affect not only your ability to run up and down a basketball court, but also your ability to absorb class lectures. But there's water in soda, right? That's true, but soda is also a diuretic, which means it pulls water out of your body. It actually makes you more dehydrated. But there's water in beer, right? Also true, but it's also a diuretic. The hops that make your beer so tasty also stimulate your kidneys to get rid of excess water. That's why whenever you "break the seal," you'll pee another one hundred times before the night's over. Dehydration is also what leads to hangovers. The less water in your system, the more messed up you feel the next day after drinking. So if you're going to have a fun-filled night of drinking, be sure to drink plenty of water during the day, and also drink a glass or two of water every couple of hours while you're out. It's a lot cheaper than alcohol and will go a long way toward preventing migraines and vomiting.

Go Work Out

There are few times in life when you have a free place to exercise and plenty of time to do it. Take advantage of it. Exercise will boost your immune system, help you avoid the freshman fifteen, and just generally make you feel better. It can also do wonders for your self-esteem. You don't have to be a gym rat, but you need to go at least three times per week. Get into a regular routine and stick to it. Track your progress with pictures or keep a training log. It might sound a little cheesy, but it's nice to see where you started compared to where you eventually get. Make sure to keep your routine balanced. Don't spend all your time on the stationary bike or every day doing bench press. Balance cardio with lifting weights, and spend different days on different muscle groups. Don't know what you're doing? Take a class on weight lifting or aerobics. You'll learn everything you need to know to get started and actually get credit doing it. Oh, and don't go just to socialize. It's easy to spend an hour in the gym and only do twenty minutes of work. Stay focused, get your workout done, and wait until you're finished to talk to that cute girl or guy on the treadmill. (And don't forget to stretch.)

Flip-Flops

If you're going to be using a community bathroom, you need to buy a cheap pair of flip-flops you don't mind throwing away at the end of the year. Remember, you're standing in what other people just washed off, and the last thing you want to do is step in a big puddle of somebody else. Flip-flops will also help you avoid athlete's foot and any other fungus or ailment of the feet. Just be sure to throw them away before you move out. There are some things soap can't wash off.

Beware the Wandering Drunk

Drunk people can be a lot of fun to watch, but they can also be extremely stupid and harmful. Beware. They've been known to attack parked cars, put couches in trees, and assault other people for very little reason at all. You don't have to totally avoid random drunk people; they can be a good source of amusement. But be aware that they can snap at any time.

The Student Health Center

The on-campus medical center is a great alternative to the emergency room. Whether you sprain an ankle or contract swine flu, the on-campus medical staff should be able to help in a reasonably short time. The health center shouldn't replace your usual doctor, but it's a good place to go on short notice. It's also a good place to get discreetly tested for STDs. And, if you don't want to pay for condoms, they'll probably give you some for free. Just make sure you know where the building is before you get sick. The last thing you need to do is wander around campus infecting other people.

Campus Security

Know the campus security number by heart. You never know when there will be an emergency, and you don't need to waste time trying to remember what number to call. Calling 911 will work, but campus security can respond faster than local services. They'll also escort you to your car or dorm late at night. *There is no reason to ever be alone.* If you don't feel comfortable traversing the parking deck at 2:00 AM, call the campus security number and wait for someone to walk with you. I know it sounds over the top, but it's way better than ending up in a tragic situation. (If you want to know your campus's crime statistics for recent years, visit ope.ed.gov/security.)

Bad Things Happen

Terrible, terrible things can happen on campus. Assault, rape, wrecks, and robberies happen every day to people who were sure it wouldn't happen to them. Have a strategy to deal with anything life throws at you before it happens. Keep a card in your wallet that tells your blood type and who to call in case of an emergency. God forbid you would ever need it, but you need to be ready just in case. If you witness something tragic, don't freak out. Stay calm, act fast, and get help.

Sleep

Morning or Evening Person?

Are you a morning or an evening person? Do you jump out of bed in the morning ready to face the day? Or do you crawl out and head straight for the coffee pot? Whichever type you are, plan your schedule accordingly. Don't sign up for classes at eight o'clock in the morning if you usually go to bed at 3:00 AM and struggle to get up before eleven. Don't schedule night classes if your best work is done during the day. Play to your strengths.

Naps

College is where the nap gets redefined. It's no longer something you hate; instead, it's something you look forward to. Naps can give you a boost of energy and help you recoup some lost sleep. You might even be inclined to schedule your classes around a daily nap. But don't overdo it. Don't nap more than forty-five minutes. Any longer than that can keep you awake at night and mess up your natural sleep cycle.

Never Study in Bed

Studying in bed will only lead to one thing: sleep. You've hardwired your brain to want to sleep whenever you crawl under the covers, so don't be surprised when you wake up with your book draped over your stomach.

Study Before the Night Before

Waiting until the night before the test to look at your notes or crack open your book will not only lead to poor grades, but it will also give you a sleep debt which will take a night or two of really good sleep to pay off. The odds are that you won't get a really good night of sleep for a while, which means your sleep debt will continue to increase. And the more tired you get, the harder it will be for you to recall what you studied. Start studying early, and get a good night's sleep before a big test. Not doing so can lead to a vicious cycle of sleep deprivation that will wreak havoc on your grades.

How Much Sleep?
You need at least eight hours of sleep per night. I realize that it's sometimes impossible to get that much, but you should strive for it nonetheless. Not getting enough sleep will make you more susceptible to illness, increase your stress levels, and can even make you fatter. (People who don't sleep much tend to eat a lot more; the longer you're awake, the more opportunities you have to stuff your face.) And catching up on sleep in class is a terrible idea. Not only do you miss the notes and assignments for the day, but also professors don't view sleeping in class very fondly. They usually remember it when you need a couple of extra points on your final grade.

Don't sleep too much, either. Sleeping twelve hours can make you feel just as crappy as sleeping four. It will make you considerably less productive and make you feel lethargic for the rest of the day. Too much sleep will also lower your immune system and has been linked to diabetes, heart disease, and chronic headaches. When your body isn't awake for long enough, it doesn't absorb enough sunlight, get enough nutrients, or experience enough exercise. So if you wake up tired, the last thing you should do is go back to sleep. Get up and do some pushups or jumping jacks to boost your temperature and get your blood circulating. (It takes a while to get your temperature up in the morning, which is why you wake up feeling drowsy. The sun also plays a huge part in the cycle, as it lowers the melatonin levels you've built up during the night. That's why it's harder to get going on dreary days.) Getting just the right amount of sleep is the key to a healthy immune system and leads to a better sense of overall well-being.

Stress

Stress and Your Body

Here are some ways in which key systems react.

Nervous System.

When stressed-physically or psychologically-the body suddenly shifts its energy sources to fighting off the perceived threat. The nervous system signals the adrenal glands to release adrenaline and cortisol. These hormones make the heart beat faster, raise blood pressure, change the digestive process and boost glucose levels in the bloodstream. (Once the crisis passes, body systems usually return to normal.)

Musculoskeletal System.

Under stress, muscles tense up. The contraction of muscles for extended periods can trigger tension headaches, migraines and various musculoskeletal conditions.

Respiratory System.

Stress can make you breathe harder and cause rapid breathing which can bring on panic attacks in some people.

Cardiovascular System.

Acute stress- stress that is momentary- causes an increase in heart rate and stronger contractions of the heart. Blood vessels that direct blood to the large muscles and to the heart dilate, increasing the amount of blood pumped to these parts of the body. Repeated episodes of acute stress can cause inflammation in the coronary arteries, thought to lead to heart attack.

Gastrointestinal System.
Stress may prompt you to eat much more or much less than you usually do. If you eat more or different foods or increase your use of tobacco or alcohol, you may experience heartburn or acid reflux. Your stomach can react with "butterflies" or even nausea or pain and may lead to vomiting. Stress has also been linked to diarrhea in some people and constipation in others.

Reproductive System.
In men, excess amounts of cortisol can affect the normal functioning of the reproductive system. Chronic stress can impair testosterone and sperm production and cause impotence. In women, stress can cause absent or irregular menstrual cycles or more painful periods. It can also reduce sexual desire.

When It Happens
When stress happens, the best thing you can do is relax. I know that's insanely difficult sometimes, but you need to slow down your breathing and chill out. Stressing out and worrying have never solved a single problem. It only makes things worse. Go exercise instead of eating. It'll make you feel better and you won't gain weight (which tends to lead to more stress). Exercise will also help you sleep better, which will make you better able to deal with what's stressing you out. Think positively and stop focusing on the worst possible outcome of whatever situation is causing you

stress. Life will go on. The sun will come out tomorrow. And no matter what's going on, this too shall pass.

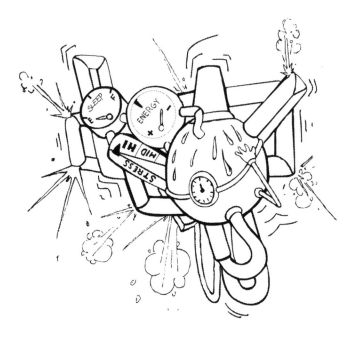

3: MONEY

*I*f you can figure out how to efficiently spend money now, you stand a good chance of being very well-off later. Knowing where to buy, what to buy, and how to pay are some of the most important things to learn in college, and figuring out how to use money now will lay the foundation for the rest of your life. The best way to become a millionaire is to start saving and spending wisely when you're young. (Here's a phrase you need to know by heart. Say it with me: "if it's free, give me three.")

Eat for Free

Anytime you get the opportunity to eat for free, you need to take it. Your dorm has pizza downstairs for a fire safety program? Go listen to the firefighter. A fraternity is hosting a cookout? Go grab a burger. Your parents are in town? Let them treat you to a nice restaurant. Eating for free allows you to spend money on other things, such as gas and concert tickets. You can also save that money and not spend it at all. (There's a shocking idea.) The fact of the matter is that you need to eat for free as often as you get the chance. Even if it means going to a boring program, hanging out with people you don't know, or listening to your mom's stories about her new cat, you need to go because *it's free*.

Use Coupons

There are billions of coupons floating around college campuses. You can seriously find a discount on nearly anything you want to buy, and you need to take advantage of these. Most universities give out free coupon books at the beginning of each semester. Take forty of them. Keep them in your book bag. Stash some in your car. Put a couple of them in your pocket before you leave home every day. Saving two dollars per day during lunch may not seem like a lot, but that adds up to hundreds of dollars by the end of the semester. Clothing stores also offer discounts through coupons. Find a dress you want? There's probably a coupon that will give you 15 percent off; you just have to find it. Have a date but low on cash? Find a coupon with those magical words "buy one, get one free." (If your date gets offended, go home early. If a person doesn't like you when you're broke, you can't trust him or her when you're rich.) Coupons can save you a ton of money. To not use them is just plain ignorant.

Seek Out the Five-Dollar Buffets

In the first few weeks of class, figure out where you can eat all you want for five dollars or less. If you're lucky, there's a cheap pizza parlor or a good Chinese place close to campus. Find a place to eat cheap in every genre of food. That way, no matter what you're craving, you know where to get it at a cost-effective price.

On-Campus Ministries

You need to seek out the on-campus ministries and find out when they do lunch. A lot of them provide home cooked meals one day per week and only charge a few bucks for it. Plus, the various denominations tend to have their meetings on different days, which means you can eat a good lunch for cheap on multiple afternoons. But you don't believe in their beliefs? Who cares? This is college. It's okay to hang around people with different beliefs. Plus, good food for cheap is something we can all believe in.

Don't Order Drinks from Restaurants

Any time you go out to eat or order fast food, don't order a drink; *get water*. It's usually free and will rarely cost more than a quarter. Asking for water is the easiest way to save money while eating out. Restaurants will usually charge two or three dollars for a drink, which again doesn't sound like much, but when it's added up, it turns out to make a huge difference in your bank account. Don't like the taste of water? Then buy one of those big boxes of flavor packets. Surely there's at least one flavor you like. (Oh, and drinking water won't make you fat.)

Take Your Own Snacks

The markup on vending machine snacks is ridiculous, so take your own. Grab some fruit from the cafeteria, make a PB&J, or buy a big pack of peanut butter crackers. Just carry some source of nourishment in your bag. It's also wise to carry a bottle of water with you. Drink machines are even worse on markup. Just remember, vending machines are expensive; food from home is cheap.

Make Your Own Coffee

Coffee can be stupidly expensive, so stopping by the coffee shop every day can do some damage to your wallet. To counteract the cost of your caffeine addiction, brew your own. Go buy an inexpensive coffeemaker, and start getting up in time to make it. Some models even come with a programmable timer, so your coffee can start brewing before you even wake up. Is there one specific latte you like? Then get on the Internet and figure out how to make it yourself. It's probably not that hard, and it'll save you a crap ton of money.

Watch Your Weight

At first, you might think my warning to watch your weight belongs in the health section. But the thing is, **_new clothes are expensive_**. If you can't fit into your clothes anymore, it could cost you some serious cash. Even if you get some great deals, replacing a wardrobe is going to take money away from everything else. So be mindful of your waistline. It's not just a health thing. Gaining a bunch of weight puts stress on your wallet, as well.

Be a DD (Designated Driver)
Drunk people will pay you to drive them around, so be a DD and earn some cash. Just act like you don't want to do it, and tell them you're almost out of gas. Usually, they'll offer you money. But make sure the amount is enough to cover gas and still have some left over. The idea here is to make a profit. Now, I'm not saying you should swindle your friends. But your car and sobriety are valuable things, and you deserve to be paid for your services. However, there is some risk. Drunk people have a tendency to throw up, so it's not a bad idea to carry vomit bags in your glove box. It's way better than having to spend hours cleaning your floorboards. Drunk people are also usually loud, obnoxious, and sometimes downright annoying. But they tend to over tip, so this whole designated driver thing can actually work out really well. Plus, alcohol is really expensive, so if you spend the whole night drinking water and then get paid to cart your friends around, you save money to make money. It's not a bad deal.

Quarters
Quarters are an extremely hot commodity. Especially if you have to pay to do laundry or want to park downtown, you're going to need bucketfuls to get through the semester. And washing machines and parking meters usually *only* take quarters; so there's no getting by with dimes and nickels. *Get quarters early.* The change machine only breaks when *you* need it. You can only flip over the couch cushions so many times before that well runs dry. So whenever you get a quarter, put it in a jar, and also be sure

to have some in your car. Doing this will help you get pretty far. (Sorry about the rhyming; I just couldn't help myself. But seriously, treat quarters like gold.)

Spare Change

Speaking of quarters in jars, it's a good idea to put *all* spare change in a jar. (Just put the quarters in a separate jar so they're easier to find.) Any time you receive change when you buy something, take it home and put it up. Holding on to four cents may seem like a waste of time, but over the course of the semester, that spare change can turn into an emergency fund. (I once paid a delinquent cable bill out of a change jar. Of course, the cable company didn't particularly like being paid in nickels; but it got paid, didn't it?)

Credit Cards

It's amazing how such small pieces of plastic can ruin your life so quickly. It's a good idea to have one; emergencies come up. But using one every day can be a terrible thing. The funny thing about credit card companies is they want their money back, and they would really like some more money on top of it. So if you do use a card to buy something, make sure you pay it off *that month*. Otherwise, the interest can make that new TV cost a lot more than it's worth. And don't just assume the Credit Card Act is going to protect you. There are a number of loopholes credit card companies have found, and in some cases they can raise your rate to as much as 29.99 percent. The best rule is to only use the card when you absolutely must. If you really want that new flat screen, save up the money to buy it. It'll mean a lot more to you. (Also, beware of signing up for credit cards on campus. Credit card companies love to take advantage of college students, so do research and find the best one before you make a commitment.)

Lending

Letting the girl down the hall borrow the *Hannah Montana: The Movie* is not a big deal. (Just make sure you get it back. College students are really good at borrowing movies indefinitely.) But letting someone borrow your car? Now, that can turn into a truly horrendous situation. Insurance companies get really weird when someone not on the policy wrecks a vehicle. Now the insurance company should pay for the damages as long as the friend had your permission to drive, but the key word there is *should*. However, it may take them weeks to investigate the accident and clear everything up. So while they take their sweet time, you're bumming rides to class because of an accident you weren't even involved in. Awesome. So when lending, ask yourself how big a deal it would be if the item gets lost, stolen, or damaged. If the risk is too great, don't lend it out. It doesn't matter how cute the person is.

Avoid Cash Advance Stores

It might be tempting to get an advance on your next paycheck, but avoid cash advance stores. Perhaps there's an emergency, and you need money ten minutes ago. Or maybe there's only one pair of shoes left in your size in the whole mall. Whatever the case may be, stay away from these loan stores. They seem like a good idea. They often offer "deals" to college students. But trust me, the mob charges lower interest. Getting one paycheck early might take you three paychecks to pay off, and that's just not worth it. If something comes up, and you need money right now, this very instant, first make sure you *really* need it right now, this very instant. And if it is a dire need, either call home or ask friends for help. If you don't want to do that, many schools offer short-term emergency loans, so go talk to the bursar's office.

Call the Bank Before You Move
Let your bank know you're moving before you actually move. Otherwise, your debit card might be declined when you try to use it in a new city. Don't hold up the checkout line because your card doesn't work and then get a phone call ten minutes later from your bank's anti-fraud officer asking if it's really you. Save yourself some frustration. Call ahead of time. Plus, they need to know where to send your statements. (This also applies to credit cards, so let them know you moved, too.)

Grants and Scholarships
Apply for every grant and scholarship you can find. Even if tuition isn't coming out of your own pocket, seek out and make a claim to the money that's out there. One of the most selfish things you can do is say, "Well, I'm not paying for it; why should I care?" You should care for three reasons: 1. It's the right thing to do. 2. It's an opportunity for you to grow up and start thinking about someone else for a change. 3. Your parents might even be inclined to spend the money they save on something for you anyway. So get on the university's Web site, find all the scholarships you qualify for, and then *apply for them*. Go by the scholarship office and ask someone what other grants and scholarships are out there, and then *apply for those*, too. Go online, find even more opportunities to apply

for, and then **apply for them**, as well. The applications usually don't take very long, and they can get you thousands of dollars in free money.

Taxes

The sooner you and your parents get taxes done, the sooner you can get money from the government. Oh, and the longer you wait, the less money you get. It's really that simple. The FAFSA money starts out as this enormous wad of cash. The government gives it out in the form of grants as students apply and show a need. But when the wad of cash is gone, **it's gone**. There is no opportunity to say, "Sorry I was late, but can you make an exception?" To avoid that situation, get your taxes done as soon as you get your W-2. Then stay on your parents about getting theirs done, too. As soon as all that is done, fill out the FAFSA online.

FAFSA

To fill out the FAFSA, visit fafsa.gov. **It's free.** If a Web site ever tries to charge you for filling out the FAFSA, **it's a scam**. It's not hard to fill out; the government has made everything clear and easy to understand. **Hold on to your pin.** Put it in a place where you'll know just where to look when you need it again a year from now. Nothing's worse than being ready to fill everything out and then having to wait on a new pin. Once the government application is done, visit your university's financial aid Web site and see if you have to fill out a form for your school, as well. Most schools require it, and you will most likely have to send it in before the government will process anything. Waiting to fill out your school's forms will decrease how much money you get, so submit all of these forms as soon as you can.

Loans

Most people can't pay for everything with grants and scholarships, and you're more than likely going to have to take out some loans. It's not a bad thing; just understand what you're getting into. First of all, you want your loans to be *subsidized*. That means they don't accrue interest while you're still in school. You may end up having to take out some unsubsidized loans, but do your best to keep those to a minimum. Don't over borrow. Take out only what you really need. Eventually, the bank will want that money back. So think long and hard before you use a student loan to buy a new big screen. And most importantly, make sure you read everything and know what's required by the loan. Learn everything about it; don't just assume they're going to tell you what you need to know. Don't let someone else know more about your money than you do.

Jobs

You have the rest of your life to work, so it's best for you to focus on your degree. However, you can't get that degree, or eat for that matter, without money. So if you must get a job, make sure you have an understanding boss. Find something with flexible hours that won't have you exhausted by the time you get home. Having money is nice, but it's not time to live large. Work enough to pay your bills and expenses, but don't work a billion hours just because you want a new car. Your grades will suffer. If you can, get a campus job. The hours are good. The bosses understand. And the pay is decent. Plus, you can walk out of class and right into work without having to go too far. Being an RA (residential advisor) is an especially good idea. You get to work in the same building you live in, which cuts down greatly on travel time, and usually your housing is completely free.

It also gives you the opportunity to get to know a lot of people and even help some of them. (Plus, you get to move in first.)

Sell Your Ticket

Need some money? Do you go to a big time football or basketball school? Do you have a student ticket? Then you've got premium merchandise. Get on Facebook. Post a flyer on a bulletin board. Just get the word out and sell the thing. Look at what other people are selling their tickets for and charge five dollars less. Just make sure to charge a deposit if you're afraid of losing your ID card. If it costs fifty dollars to replace a lost card, you're probably not going to come out ahead. (And if you're really smart, you'll make friends with a player on the team who can hook you up with another ticket.)

Losing Keys Is Losing Money

If you live in a dorm or apartment, you probably can't make copies of your key. That means losing it can cost you some major dollars. Losing it also sometimes means the lock has to be replaced, which can cost you even more money. So don't be careless with it. Fasten it to something that makes it hard to lose. Many put it on a lanyard. It's also a good idea to attach your name and phone number to it. (Don't put your address on it; if the wrong person found it, you would make it kind of easy to rob you.) Plus, it sucks having to wait for your roommate to get back; if you live by yourself, then it really sucks.

Dumpster Dive

A lot of college students are spoiled and have little appreciation for what their parents buy them, so when the school year is over, they tend to throw everything away. Instead of donating to Goodwill or making more than one trip, they just put it all in the dumpster. That means right after finals is the best time to find extremely valuable and useful free stuff if you are willing to dumpster dive. Now, people are going to look at you like you're an idiot. Climbing into dumpsters isn't exactly the most socially acceptable thing to do, but when it yields you a brand new computer desk or big screen TV, who cares what other people think? If you're too cool to climb into dumpsters, that's fine. But don't whine about how nothing good ever happens to *you* when your more adventurous friend comes home with a brand new living room set. Dumpster diving is like treasure hunting. You have to dig to find anything. Just make sure to wash your hands. (True story: the fifty-two-inch TV in my living room right now came out of a dumpster, and it works great.)

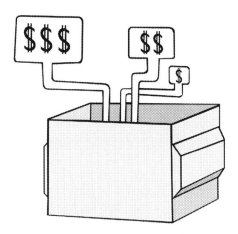

Books

Cost

Books are expensive. That's just the way it is. Get over it. Some majors require a bunch of small, cheap books that add up to a lot. Some majors require a few huge books that are hundreds of dollars apiece. Either way, you're probably going to have to shell out some major cash at the beginning of each semester. However, there are a lot of ways to save some money. If you become a smart shopper, your wallet won't take as big a hit. And you just might break even when you sell the books back. (Oh, and the average college student spends twice as much on alcohol as he does on books, so you probably shouldn't complain about the price of books too much.)

Buy Used

Buy used books whenever you can. It's not like buying a used DVD player. The used books are usually better than the new ones. Why? Because other people have already made notes in them. Flip through the book to see if key points have been highlighted; don't buy a book that has too much highlighting. Some people don't understand that it's useless to highlight everything. You'll save money by buying an older edition, but make sure you know how much has changed or been added. Sometimes publishers just update the pictures and change a few paragraphs; sometimes they overhaul the whole book. Used books are also a good bit cheaper, and you'll get the same amount back as you would for a new book of the same edition when you sell it later.

Shop Around

Be an informed shopper and shop around. Don't get to class only to find out other people bought the same book for twenty dollars cheaper. Call bookstores around town and find out their prices. Look online and compare costs. Being patient can save you some serious money. Web sites such as Amazon.com, Textbooks.com, and Half.com can save you so much it's sad. Just be aware of where the book is being shipped from. A book coming from the other side of the country is obviously going to take longer to get to you, so it might be worth spending a few more dollars on a book if it's going to be shipped from a much closer location. And especially make sure the book isn't being shipped from a store that's just right up the road; don't receive the book a week later and learn it came from the same zip code. (That's embarrassing.)

Shop Early

Bookstores will sometimes offer deals on buying your books early. So if there are books on your list that you absolutely know you have to have, take advantage of ordering early. Shopping early also means that any books you buy online will get there in time for class. Don't miss homework assignments because you ordered the book too late.

Wait

If there are some books on your syllabi that you're not sure you'll need, then wait to buy them. Professors often get into a course and decide to go another direction; so definitely wait before buying books used later in the semester. Now, this tactic does come with some risk. The bookstores can run out of the book, and shipping can sometimes take forever; so make sure you're friends with someone in class who can let you borrow her copy. And make sure you're not going to drop the class before you buy all of the books for it. (Also, if you don't have the money to buy a book and can't borrow it, just go to the bookstore and do your assignment there. Don't make it obvious or anything, but the worst they can do is to ask you to leave.)

Theft

Book theft is pretty common. Especially around the end of the semester, when people get strapped for cash, textbooks start to disappear. Treat your books like money. You wouldn't leave forty dollars just lying on the table while you went to the bathroom, so don't leave your books there, either. Finals are stressful enough; you don't need your books stolen a day before the test. Don't be careless and allow someone else to steal and sell your books back. That's **your** money.

Investments

There are some things that you really just need to spend the money on.

Towels

Buy some high quality towels that will last you throughout your college career. Get the big, soft ones. They just make life feel better.

Pillow

Stress can put serious cricks in your neck. Don't use a pillow that does the same. A good night's sleep is super important, so buy a pillow that helps you accomplish that.

Mattress Pad

Dorm beds aren't the most comfortable. A mattress pad will make it feel more like home.

Mace

If you're concerned about being attacked, buy a can of mace that you can clip to your key ring. Just remember that it's no good in your backpack. If you're nervous about the parking deck at night, keep the mace in your hand.

Microwave Cookbook

It's important to be able to cook your own food. It'll save you money, and it's honestly not that hard. But you might not have regular access to a stove, so get a microwave cookbook. There are dishes in there you might not have known you could make in the microwave.

Cleats

If you're going to do any outdoor intramurals, you need a good pair of cleats. Cheap cleats will save you money, but maybe not your ankles. Find a pair that is comfortable and will last you a good long while.

Cell Phone Case

A new cell phone is expensive. Buy a case for it made of hard plastic. You're going to drop it; it's gonna happen. So make sure it's protected.

Tool Kit

Get a tool kit with basic tools in it. You never know when something will break or when you'll have to put a project together. Just keep it in a place where you'll remember its whereabouts.

Flashlight

The power tends to go out a few times per year. Keep a good flashlight in your room so you won't have to stumble to the bathroom. Also make sure it has fresh batteries.

Bike

A bicycle will get you around campus super fast. It turns a fifteen-minute walk into a three-minute ride. But you get what you pay for. Don't expect a cheap bike to last more than a year. It won't take long for the brakes to wear out and for the gears to stop working right. And if you ever wreck a cheap bike, it will probably break beyond repair.

Calendar

Buy a calendar that makes you smile, and use it to remember upcoming test and due dates. Go through it and put all important dates on it. Your grandmother will appreciate it when you remember her birthday.

Futon

Futons were invented for college students. It's a couch when you want to watch a movie. It's a bed when you have a friend over from out of town.

Calculator

Many classes require the use of a calculator, and professors ***won't*** let you use your phone. Get a quality calculator and keep up with it.

A Good Nerf Gun

A Nerf gun is a very useful thing to have. You never know when a Nerf war will break out, and you don't want to be unprepared. Buy extra darts, though. You're probably going to lose a few.

Air Fresheners

College will introduce you to a whole new world of smells that you didn't even realize existed. Stock up on products that will help you triumph in the fight against stink.

4: Food

F ood is one of the biggest challenges when you get to college. You have to get used to the fact that your folks aren't there to cook for you, and the money for food now most likely comes out of your own pocket. If you get to the end of the semester and realize you don't have any money left, it probably went into your stomach. Learning to balance the cost and nutrition of food is an often overlooked skill that can greatly enhance your college experience. And remember, if you're doing a program or event that involves college students, they go where the food is. Having a lot of food can usually mean having a lot of them show up.

Ramen Noodles

When it comes to price, you can't beat ramen noodles. For a few pennies, you can have a small meal that doesn't taste half bad. There's not a lot of nutritional value in it, and it's extremely high in sodium. But when you need to eat fast and don't have any money, it's the way to go. To put a little more sustenance in it, add a scrambled egg.

Peanut Butter and Jelly

For a good meal between classes, the PB&J is a solid choice. It only takes a few minutes to make, and it's actually pretty filling. To expedite the process, get the squeeze bottle jelly that's easier to spread. And to put a little something extra in it, add some honey to the peanut butter. It'll give it a slightly sweeter taste and add a small boost of energy. Be aware that peanut butter is pretty high in fat, so eating five sandwiches per day probably isn't a good idea.

Energy Drinks

Energy drinks should be good pick-me-ups, not dietary staples. They're not exactly the healthiest things you can put in your body, but they can provide some much needed energy if your sleeping habits have been less than stellar. Just remember, the more you drink, the less effective they are, and they can lead to a serious crash. Don't drink them too close to bedtime, as they will interfere with your sleeping habits. (Get the sugar free cans to make them a little healthier.)

Soft Drinks

Soft drinks are high in calories and, even worse, high in sugar. They cause tooth decay and disrupt sleep. They're associated with obesity and diabetes and have even been linked to heart disease. The debate over high-fructose corn syrup is still going on, but odds are that it's not a good thing to put inside you. Your body can handle soft drinks once in a while, but drinking them every day can lead to some serious weight gain. They've also been found to be addictive, so the more you drink, the more you're going to want.

Cereal

Cereal is pretty much the go-to meal. It's good any time of the day. You can eat it dry or with milk (or with water, if you so desire). And there are a billion different flavors to choose from. Just realize how much sugar is in what you're eating. To make it a little healthier, fill half the bowl with something healthy like plain Cheerios and pour the sugary cereal on top of it. You'll still get the taste, but with half the sugar.

Meal Plans

Most universities require freshmen to have meal plans, and they make a lot of money off people leaving money in their accounts. At the end of the year, if you haven't used up all the money on your plan, it disappears. Don't just give your money away. I realize the selection on campus might not be the best. Get over it. You've already paid for it, so you might as well eat it. If you get to the end and realize you won't be able to use up all the money, just start buying other people's meals. And don't be ashamed to take food from the cafeteria for later. Throw some fruit in your bag to eat after class.

Dollar Menus

When you're low on funds, dollar menus are a great way to get food on the cheap. However, eating from the dollar menu too often will put you well on your way to the freshman fifteen. The healthy menu items tend to cost more than a dollar, and people tend to order more food because "it's just a dollar," so they end up consuming more calories. Don't eat fast food more than once per day, and the earlier you eat it, the better, as it gives your body more time to burn it off. (If you can avoid fast food altogether, you'll probably live longer.)

The Grocery Store

Never go to the grocery store hungry. You'll end up buying a bunch of food that will probably go bad before you get around to actually eating it. And buy store brands. They usually taste just as good as the name brands, but they cost a lot less (especially when it comes to cereal). Buy in bulk. The initial cost is more, but you save a lot over time. However, only buy the things in bulk that you eat or drink a lot of. You lose the savings if the food goes bad before you eat it. And look at the unit prices. The cost per ounce or per pound will show you the best value. Buying the biggest container doesn't always mean saving the most money.

Air

Before closing up packages of food, get rid of as much of the air as possible. Bread, cereal, and potato chips will last a lot longer if there's no air in the bag. Use clothespins or twist ties to keep the air out.

Fruit

Fruit gives you energy. Eat lots of it. It's inexpensive, and you don't have to prepare it. Plus, it fits easily into a book bag. But when you're storing it, be sure to keep it separated. Fruit releases ethylene, a gas that speeds up ripening and causes other fruit to release even more ethylene, which leads to even more rapid ripening. It sounds strange, but separating fruit makes it last longer.

Breakfast

Eat breakfast. You don't have to eat a lot, but eat something. Breakfast sets up your metabolism for the rest of the day. If you don't eat anything in the morning, your body thinks it's not going to eat anything for the rest of the day. So when you do give it food, it stores more of it. You don't need that. By eating breakfast, you're telling your body to go ahead and start burning calories because there's more where that came from. A lot of people failing at losing weight don't eat breakfast. They don't realize they're sabotaging themselves.

Vitamins

It's hard to get all the vitamins and minerals you need, so find a good multivitamin and take it every day. It's better to get your vitamins from food, but just getting them at all is a good thing. Find one that says "easy on stomach," and if you can find one that tastes good, you're more likely to actually take it. Take them right after you work out. Your body absorbs them a lot better in the hour after exercise.

The Freshman Fifteen

You don't have to be a victim. You don't have to move in with one pant size and move out with another. Just watch what you eat. Limit your portions on high calorie foods, and avoid fast food whenever you can. Make sure you eat breakfast, and exercise a few days per week. Join some intramural teams, and don't shy away from the gym. Oh, you've heard all of this before? That's because there's no secret formula. There's no magic to this. And the freshman fifteen can easily become the freshman thirty. It doesn't have to, though. You just have to take control over what you put in your body.

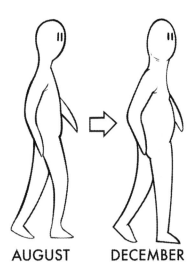

AUGUST   DECEMBER

Fat Cells

According to Dr. Sanjay Gupta over at *CNNhealth.com*[2], once your body creates fat cells, they never go away. They can deflate, but they're impossible to get rid of. (That's why it's so easy to gain the weight back after you lose it.) So, all the fat cells you create now are going to be with you for the rest of your life. By gaining fifteen pounds your first semester, you're setting yourself up to gain even more weight later. But let's say you start working out and lose the fifteen pounds in the second semester. Well, you've emptied those fat cells, but they are ready and willing to be filled back up again. Your body is going to naturally gain weight as you age. That's just part of life. But you don't have to jump-start the process when you're eighteen.

Still Hungry?[3]

MensHealth.com published an article that sheds light on why you might still be hungry after a meal.

Too Much High-Fructose Corn Syrup
Fructose has been found to impede leptin, the hormone that tells your body when it's had enough to eat. Drinking too much soda or tea can make your body think it's still hungry long after you're full.

Canned Food
Canned foods are high in bisphenol-A, which can cause abnormal surges of leptin that lead to food cravings and obesity.

Too Small a Breakfast
Eating a big breakfast makes for smaller rises in blood sugar and insulin throughout the day, meaning fewer sudden food cravings.

You're Dehydrated

Dehydration often mimics the feeling of hunger. If you've just eaten and still feel hungry, drink a glass of water before eating more, and see if your desires don't diminish.

Not Enough Green Leafy Vegetables

Leafy greens are rich in the essential B-vitamin folate and help protect against depression, fatigue, and weight gain. They are also high in vitamin K, another insulin-regulating nutrient that helps suppress cravings.

Boredom

When there's nothing else to do, people tend to eat. If you're just sitting around and get hungry, get up and do something to take your mind off food. If the hunger goes away, you really just needed something to do.

How Long Common Foods Last

Bread

It depends on the temperature, humidity, and preservatives in it, but bread should last around a week. However, once one piece gets moldy, the whole loaf has mold growing in it. ***Do not consume it.***

Spaghetti

Spaghetti with meat sauce can be safely kept in the fridge for three to four days.

Hamburger
Cooked hamburger meat will last three or four days. Raw hamburger will last no more than two or three days. If it starts to lose its color and stinks, throw it out.

Chicken
Cooked chicken could be good up to four days. Raw chicken is best used within one or two days.

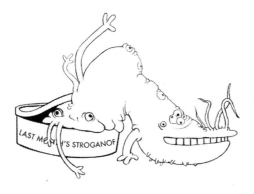

Steak
Cooked steak could be good up to four or five days. Raw steak is best used within one or two days.

Fish
Cooked fish is good for about one day. Raw fish is best used within three days.

Cookies
Cookies will last up to two weeks if you keep them in a sealed container.

Leftovers

Leftovers need to go in the fridge within two hours of serving to reduce the risk of food-borne illnesses. Bacteria grow more quickly at room temperature, so put the food in the fridge as soon as you're done with it. For larger items, refrigerate your leftovers in a bunch of small containers to avoid large clumps. That way, the food will cool quicker and more evenly. A large clump increases the chance of something growing in the center because it didn't cool properly. Leftovers should last three to four days.

5: PEOPLE

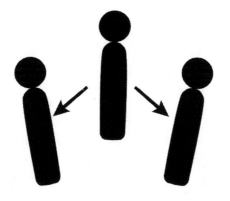

*P*eople make college fun to look back on. The relationships you make over the next four to seven years will influence the rest of your life. And whom you know and how you get along with them greatly affects not only your overall well-being, but also your likelihood of graduation. Getting to know the right people now is going to pay huge dividends later.

How You're Treated

Don't be surprised when people treat you how you act. No one has any previous knowledge of you. All they know is what you do. If you act like a slut, people are going to assume you're a slut and will treat you as such. If you act stuck-up, they're going to assume you're stuck-up. If you act like a person who has it all together, they're going to assume you do in fact have it all together. It's not a hard concept. As mentioned in the first chapter of this book, college gives you the awesome ability to reinvent yourself. Take the opportunity and be exactly who *you* want to be.

Meet Everybody

It's not time to be shy; you need to get out of your room as much as possible and meet everybody you can. College life is not going to come to you, and most likely, people aren't, either. So, get out there. Go to art shows and basketball games. Go to video game tournaments and religion debates. Go to everything. That's where the people are. Meeting more people means making more connections, which means knowing more folks who can help you get a job. Especially go to stuff during the first couple of weeks of school; the people you meet during the first couple of weeks will help unlock your next four to seven years. And go to events you're not really interested in. You'll meet some cool people who probably don't have much in common with you, but you might end up being more similar than you think.

Be Polite

Fewer things will get you farther in college than politeness. It'll get you better grades. It'll get you faster attention from secretaries. It'll get you more food in the cafeteria. Being polite encourages people to help you. It's not hard; and it doesn't cost you a dime.

Saying thank you, yes sir, or no ma'am is free of charge. I realize you've probably been told that for years. (And I'm not trying to sound like your parents.) But the fact of the matter is that politeness will help you get through college a lot more smoothly than any alternative.

Professors

Titles

Use Dr. or Professor—not Mr., Mrs., or Ms.—when addressing your professors. Most professors get offended if they have their doctorates and you refer to them as Mr. or Mrs., and rightly so. They spent years upon years earning those degrees and deserve to be acknowledged accordingly.

Eye Contact

Make eye contact. Don't stare out the window. Don't look at the floor. Don't watch the person in front of you chat on Facebook. Definitely don't fall asleep. Let the professor know you're paying attention. Looking at other things only encourages him to call on you. He wants to know if you're actually listening.

No Excuses

You either did the work or you didn't. Don't make up some long, drawn out story on why you didn't get things done. They've heard it before; and the previous version was better. Just do the assignments, and if you don't get them done, take responsibility for it. (Unless you've been sick; in which case you should definitely hand in a doctor's excuse. Don't lose points when you don't have to.)

Be Smart

If you haven't read the assignment or done the homework, don't make it obvious. Don't announce to the class that you didn't do the work. Just keep your head down and hope your professor doesn't call on you. Answer the first question you know and hope she won't come back to you for the rest of class.

Be Brave

If he's moving too fast, be brave and raise your hand to ask him to slow down. He won't take it personally. Professors want you to learn. They don't mind easing the pace if it ensures you don't miss important ideas. Plus, the rest of the class will probably thank you.

Office Hours

Know your professors' office hours and use them. A lot of professors would prefer to talk to you face-to-face, and their office hours are the best time to get help. Don't rely on e-mail if you have a pertinent question for your professor. She might not check her e-mail but a couple of times per day. Look on your syllabus, find out when her office hours are, and stop by and see her. Just make sure you've done the reading and homework **before** asking for help. Professors don't appreciate being mined for answers.

E-Mail

If you have a quick question or if office hours are over, e-mail is the best way to go. But don't e-mail professors in the same way you e-mail your friends. These are some highly learned individuals, so please use proper grammar and spelling. Don't write your message like a text message. Use "for" instead of "4." Show them you actually understand how to use the English language. Oh, and e-mailing them the night before a big test or paper is due is usually not a good idea. Some professors don't even check e-mail at home, and you're unlikely to get the information you need on such late notice. They also won't appreciate you waiting until the last minute.

Not Going to Class

Don't expect a lot of enthusiastic help if you don't go to class. Even in classes with no attendance policy, the professor sees who's there and who isn't. If he knows you haven't been coming, he probably won't feel inclined to help you.

Final Grades

In the end, the professor's opinion is the only one that matters. If she knows you're really trying and that you've been working hard, she'll probably help you out when final grades are posted. And don't blame the professor if you fail. This only works if 100 percent of the class fails. You get what you earn. And begging usually won't get you very far.

Outside of Class

Professors are pretty normal people. You're likely to run into them at restaurants and grocery stores. It can be uncomfortable and awkward if you allow it to be. Stay away from small talk. Stick to a quick "hello" and "see you next class" tactic. However, you should definitely get to know professors you like and interact with them outside of class. They usually have cool houses, cook good food, and know some good stories. Don't be naïve enough to think education ends in the classroom.

Roommates

Choose Wisely

Choosing the wrong roommate can seriously ruin a semester. In the dorm, you're sharing a space of shoebox proportions. In an apartment or house, you're sharing bills. In both instances, you're probably sharing a bathroom. So, a wrong choice in roommates can be detrimental to your mental and physical well-being. If you're living in the dorm, it might be best to room with a stranger. It's amazing how much more considerate strangers can be than friends. If you're in an apartment or house, sign the lease with someone who you **know** will pay his half of the bills. It doesn't matter how good of friends you are. If he has a history of missing payments, don't go into business with him. He'll miss paying the same bills with you there, too.

Friends

Here's the deal: ***Good friends don't always make good roommates, but good roommates often make good friends***. About a billion friendships have ended as a result of rooming together. Finding out the gross personal habits of another human being can be a real deal breaker. The biggest problem is that friends tend to just assume things are all right when they're not. Friends tend to act a little too comfortable around each other, which can lead to some real problems. So, if you're thinking about rooming with a really good friend, you need to really make sure it's the right decision. Being wrong can destroy your relationship.

Ground Rules
Decide on a set of ground rules **before** you need them. It will help limit misunderstandings and will provide protocol for things like bringing dates back to the room, borrowing shampoo, and eating each other's food. (If you live in the dorm, your RA can mediate and make suggestions if necessary.) So, if you don't want to get stuck taking out the trash every time or always be the one who vacuums, you should figure these details out before they become a problem. Write them all down and then sign your agreement. It sounds cheesy, but it's a useful tool when your roommate isn't pulling her weight.

Problems
If you have a problem, say something. Figure out a way to fix it. Most issues usually turn out to be simple misunderstandings, so don't bottle up your frustration. Don't complain to everyone about how terrible your roommate is. And definitely don't resort to petty revenge. **Go talk to your roommate.** Work it out; feel better about life; and move on to something more important.

Mornings and Nights
Be considerate if you're coming in late or leaving early. You don't like other people waking you up before it's time. And don't just keep on pushing snooze. Either get up or turn the alarm off. Just because it's time for you to get up doesn't mean everyone else should, too.

Borrowing
The first thing you need to remember is to ask **before** you borrow anything. Never just assume it's all right. Even if you know your

roommate won't mind, ask him anyway. Taking things without asking is extremely disrespectful and can lead to a problem. When you do borrow something, give it back in better condition. If you screw something up, buy a new one. Period.

Common Sense

Don't put a drink near your roommate's computer. Don't borrow his toothbrush. Turn your speakers down or off when he's trying to study or sleep. Pick your clothes up off the floor. And throw away trash *before* it starts to smell. Basically, use that natural common sense God gave you. (If you lack any natural common sense, please ask someone to help you.) Don't be a bad roommate because you screwed up the obvious stuff.

The First or Last Rule

When something is not yours, never be the first person to open it and never be the person who uses up the last one. Whether it's a bag of potato chips, a tube of toothpaste, or a piece of birthday cake, if you don't own it, stick to the middle. Taking the first or last can cause unnecessary conflict. (Of course, if you have direct permission, have at it.)

Parents

Adjusting

Be patient with your parents. They have to make major adjustments, too. If they're calling you twelve times per day, don't yell at them; just explain that you would appreciate it if they only called once or twice per week. College is the next step on the path toward the real world. It's a lot harder to stay on that path if they're checking in on you every day. You still need each other, just not as much as you used to.

Your Old Room

Don't be surprised if your old room goes untouched, patiently awaiting your return. Also don't be surprised if it becomes a new theater room or home office. It's all part of your parents' adjustment process. So don't be weirded out or offended. Your parents are just trying to get over the fact that you are not there.

Letters

Send home letters from time to time. Yes, real life letters. (And yes, people still actually write them.) They don't have to be long or formal or highly detailed. Just fill them in on a few things going on in your life. They'll appreciate it more than you know. Oh, and a quick hint: Don't use the letter to ask them for money. They'll be shocked.

Advice

Your parents are a wealth of information. They've probably been through some of the same things you're experiencing, and they want you to ask them questions. Don't let pride or fear of awkwardness keep you from lifesaving answers. Times have definitely changed, but don't just assume they won't have any advice that's relevant. People haven't changed that much. And they might have gone through the exact same situation you're facing right now. Just remember that calling with a complaint will send them into problem-solving overdrive, so when you just need someone to listen, make that clear.

And make sure to balance out bad stories with good ones. They only know what you tell them, so don't let every story be about how terrible life is. (And remember: If you were really that much smarter or better than them, you wouldn't have to ask them for money.)

Your Relationships

Your relationships with your parents will probably get better now that you don't have to deal with each other's crap on a daily basis. We tend to be a lot like our parents, and those similarities tend to cause problems. However, once you move out and the amount of time you're around each other is smaller, the time you are together becomes more valuable. That's not to say you won't get into any more arguments, but perhaps they won't be as frequent. Remember: we're talking about people who will support you to the end.

Grades

Show them your grades. (Especially if they're paying for everything.) They need to know you're not just partying. Prove to them that you really are cut out for college life and living on your own. If revealing your grades embarrasses you, then perhaps it's time to work a little harder. Use it as a reality check. But remember that professors never want to hear from your parents because of a bad grade. It's not going to help; all it will do is give you a bad reputation among the professors in your major.

It's Your Life

Don't let them decide your life for you. This may have worked when you were younger and wanted to watch cartoons instead of practicing piano, but it's **your** life now. You have to pursue your own goals and dreams. Listen to your parents and ask for their advice, but don't let them live vicariously through you. This is your time. Do what's best for you. But make sure you let them take you out to dinner every once in a while. You just can't beat free food. Oh, and one more thing: If they've always said you could do it, prove them right. If they've always said you'd never graduate, prove them wrong. It's that simple.

Other Really Important People

Secretaries
Be nice to secretaries. They've probably been working at the same desk for years, know the system, and can save you a lot of time and stress. They know which important papers you need to turn in and how to do pretty much everything. Being polite to them can be the difference between a stress-free afternoon and pulling your hair out.

Advisors
Be on a first name basis with your academic advisor. She'll make sure you graduate on time and don't lose thousands of dollars because you forgot to take a random biology class. But you need someone who will do more than just okay a schedule and take a hold off your account. You need someone who truly cares if you succeed. A lot of them are really just professors who were forced to double up as advisors; that means a lot of them don't actually want to do it. If you get stuck with someone who doesn't actually care about you, find someone who will. And make sure to visit your advisor's office early. She'll be less busy and more able to help you.

Study Partners

Find someone smarter than you to study with. Use Facebook to organize meetings. Don't be dead weight. Show up on time. Bring everything you need. Contribute to the discussion. Your study partner isn't there to just teach you, so don't go into it without knowing anything.

Residential Advisors

Ask your residential advisors anything. They're trained to deal with your issues. They're also older and can give you inside advice on how to deal with everything around you. They may not have all the answers, but they know the people who do. And don't make them write you up. They don't want to do it. It's annoying, and they'd much rather be doing something else. If you do something really stupid, they're going to have to call you out on it. And one more thing: **move out on time**. Don't make your RA sit around and wait on you. It could get ugly.

Tutors

If you need help, don't wait until finals week to seek it out. You know the subjects you're not good at. Find a tutor to help you through them. But don't waste his time. If you don't want to learn or do what it takes to understand the material, then please do it by yourself. The tutor could be helping someone else who actually cares about earning a good grade.

Lunch Ladies

Being friends with lunch ladies equals one thing: **more food**. Smiling at them, talking to them, and being genuinely glad to see them is the difference between three scoops and one.

That meal plan you were forced to buy was expensive; get your money's worth. Remember, friends help friends. So go be their friend.

Information Technology (IT) People
Knowing people in IT can save you an incredible amount of time, money, and sanity. Your computer could have something terribly wrong with it that an IT person can fix with just a few clicks. Repair shops will charge one hundred dollars just to look at a broken computer. An IT person might repair it for fun. She'll help you install new hardware, and she'll give you updates on all the latest technology. Knowing just one can make your life a whole lot better.

That Guy

There is a certain category of people that you really, really don't want to be classified in. I call it "that guy," but *it just as easily applies to girls.* You probably already know people who fall into the category. The major types of "that guy" are listed here:

The Video-Games-Took-Over-My-Life Guy
Flunking out because of a video game is just embarrassing. I know they're fun and all, but don't forget why you're here.

The I-Have-Sex-with-Anything-That-Moves-Guy
This quickly becomes the I-have-a-bunch-of-STDs guy. Just remember: *love fades; herpes is forever.*

The I–Argue-with-Crazy-Campus-Preachers Guy

The preacher's there to get under your skin, and if you ignore him, he might go away. Arguing with him only encourages him to be crazier. If you want to have a true theological discussion, seek out someone who isn't yelling his lungs out in the middle of the quad. Find a campus minister or local church pastor who will have an honest conversation.

The I-Have-to-Be-the-Center-of-Attention Guy

It's okay if the world doesn't revolve around you. I promise.

The I-Know-Someone-Who-Did-It-Better Guy

It's hard to have a conversation with someone who's already heard every story and apparently knows someone who did it bigger, faster, and better than you.

The Always-Better-at-It Guy

For some strange reason, I doubt you're the expert or world's greatest at everything. Call me crazy.

The I-Don't-Like-Showers Guy

Do the campus a favor. Take showers on a regular basis. It's just common decency.

The I-Don't-Do-Laundry Guy

When your dirty clothes smell, it makes your room smell, which coincidentally makes you smell. Did I mention it makes your roommate smell, too? Wash your clothes; don't wait for your folks to do it. If you don't know how, turn to chapter 11.

The I've-Got-More-Money-Than-You Guy
So your dad's a lawyer, and your mom's a doctor. No one cares.

The Ignorant Guy
When you get to college, you can't claim ignorance as an excuse anymore. Saying "well, I didn't know" after a racist or sexist comment doesn't get you off the hook. If you're one of those people who have been known to make such comments, then the next time you have a thought—let it go.

The Empty-Fridge-Container Guy
If you use up the last drop, throw it away. Don't mislead someone into thinking there's milk when there isn't any. Putting water on cereal sucks.

The Can-I-Borrow-It Guy
The more you borrow, the less people want to lend. If you do borrow something, make sure you bring it back better than you got it.

The Got-a-New-Girlfriend Guy
When you get a new girlfriend, don't forget your real friends. Doing so might make them forget you. And that makes for a very lonely life when she decides to dump you.

The Ending-Spoiler-Guy
If you've already seen the movie or finished the book, shut your freaking mouth. Don't ruin it for everybody else.

The World's-Against-Me Guy
Quit complaining. The whole world *is not* out to get you. A couple of people might be, but not the whole world.

The Religion-Sniper Guy
Religion is one of the best things to talk about when you get to college, but don't sneak it into conversations just so you can force your ideas on other people.

The Texting-While-Talking Guy
No, I love it when you stare at your lap and move your thumbs at blistering speeds while I'm talking to you. It tells me you care.

The Something's-Always-Wrong-with-Me Guy
Here's the thing: the more you think you're sick, the more likely you are to get sick, so quit reading about new diseases and imagining that you have the symptoms.

The-Conspiracy-Theory Guy
Whether it's the government or aliens, someone's covering up the truth, and somehow you're the only one who knows about it. For some reason, I don't believe you.

The Always-Wasted Guy
Always being wasted leads to always missing class, always failing, and never graduating. It also has a tendency to destroy something important: your brain.

The Porn-Is-Better-Than- a Real-Person Guy
A two-minute rollercoaster ride is a lot less work, but nothing satisfies like a relationship with a real live person. It's also really embarrassing when your roommate walks in.

The Not Strong Enough for Big Weights Guy
If you can't lift the weight more than once without help, you need to take some weight off the bar. Stop loading up the bar just so you can stare at it for ten minutes and then fail to do one rep. No one's impressed.

The My-Tan-Emits-Radiation Guy
Being tan when you're nineteen is a pretty attractive thing. Being leathery when you're thirty-five probably won't get you many dates. Take care of your skin. A baseball glove for a face is just no good.

The I'll-Do-It-Tomorrow Guy
Don't worry. It'll be here tomorrow. And the day after that. And the day after that. And the day after forever. Wait. Was that life? I think it passed you by yesterday.

Some of the most important words you can remember are these: ***don't be that guy.***

6: The Dorm

*T*he closer you live to campus, the more likely you are to go to class, and the more likely you are to graduate. To live really close to campus, it's best to live in a dorm. It's usually cheaper than an apartment, you don't have to pay utility bills, your classes are right outside your door, and it's full of people who will probably hang out with you. Dorm dwellers have even been found to make better grades. But there are a few things you need to know about living there. If you master them, the dorm might even become a second home. (That's a good thing; I swear.)

Live There

Live in the dorm at least for a little while. I realize it has some real turnoffs, such as shared bathrooms and having to coexist with another human being inside a ten-by-ten-foot box, but it has a lot more benefits. It's extremely important to learn to live with people who are nothing like you. It's equally important to learn how to take care of everything on your own, and the dorm provides a nice change from your folks do it all. But it's not as overwhelming as getting your own apartment. (Plus, you don't have to sublease a dorm room over the summer.) Dorm life gives you daily opportunities to meet and hang out with new people, and after the first couple of weeks of the semester, you can have a solid group of friends. You'll get to try a ton of new things through dorm-sponsored programs and events, and you'll never be out of the loop for on-campus activities. And best of all, if you're up at 4:00 AM, there's probably someone else there who's awake and willing to play video games or watch a movie with you. Now, you don't have to live there all four years or anything, and dorm life just isn't for some people, but you should definitely give it a try. You might enjoy it. It might even become home.

Choosing the Right One

When you visit campus, ask to take a tour through some of the dorms. Ask your guide and advisor about the various buildings, and consult your campus map before choosing. Try to get assigned to one centrally located between food and classes. If you can live in one with good parking, you are truly blessed. And if you're a freshman, don't get a private room. It's not time to be by yourself. It's time to deal with other people. Sharing a room will make you a better person—one way or another. (Be aware: some schools don't let you pick.)

Protect Your Friendships

Don't live in the same room with a really good friend. More than likely, by the end of the year, you're going to hate each other. People are naturally more polite to people they don't know. A friend tends to assume things are cool when they aren't. "It's all right if I take your laptop to my next class, right? It's cool if I put my dirty clothes on your bed, right?" You just tend not to hear those kinds of things from strangers. So, protect your friendships. It's a great idea to live in the same dorm as your friends, but it's a terrible idea to live in the same room.

Moving In

Know when your move-in day is and follow it. If you show up early, they probably won't let you in. Campus will be crazy, and parking will be hectic, so get everything out of your car as quickly as possible. Don't worry about getting your room situated until everything is in. People coming in behind you will need your parking spot, so move your vehicle as soon as you can. You're going to receive a ton of paperwork to fill out. Don't be overwhelmed. Just fill it all out and get it back to your RA. When filling out the room damage form, you really need to go through the room and check everything. Don't just assume the room is good to go and sign your name. If you don't report damages before you move in, they'll charge *you* for them when you move out. And make sure you sign everything, as it makes your RA's job a lot easier if he doesn't have to hunt you down later. Most importantly, enjoy moving in. It's chaotic, confusing, and tiresome, but it's also pretty exciting. So relax and make the most of it; you only get so many.

First Week Programs

Go to the first week programs. They're goofy. They're embarrassing. They're full of people you need to know. The relationships you create during the first week will have a huge impact on how the year turns out. And being "too cool" can also make you "too lonely" on Saturday night. *So go.* I realize a lot of them are dumb, but you're not going for the program. You're going for the people. (You could also be going for the food; there's no shame in that.) The first week activities are designed to help you get to know the other folks in the dorm and on campus. As the year progresses, you get busy, and you get fewer chances to meet people, so take advantage of your opportunities early.

Sprinklers

Don't hang anything from the sprinklers. Don't touch the sprinklers. Don't even look at the sprinklers. If you set the sprinklers off, it's going to be a very, very bad day. Not only will everything in your room be destroyed, but also everything on the rest of the floor. One sprinkler tends to set off the rest of them, so go ahead and expect to be beaten up. And the water isn't even going to be nice and clean. No, it's going to be this foul smelling, black grossness that covers everything you own. Oh, and *you* will be charged with the damages. So be smart; stay away from them.

Moving the Furniture

First of all, make sure your roommate is there before you start moving the furniture. It's not a good sign for your roommate to show up and you've already changed everything; she probably won't appreciate it. Bunking the beds or bringing in a couch should be a group decision, so don't just assume it's cool. You're going to have to share this room for the next eight months; don't start off on the wrong foot. Check with the RA before you do anything drastic, and keep in mind that most dorms have rules about removing furniture from rooms.

Realize Its Age

Most dorms were built before you were born, so don't be surprised if the wall colors are from the 70s, the carpet is from the 80s, and the smell is from ... well, who knows? You're not here for the aesthetic value of the place; you're here to sleep. With that said, you can't treat it like a brand new building. Don't overload outlets. Don't put too much weight on shelves. And don't sit on the desks. The windows might not open. The clothes rack might be hanging on by a thread. And the tiles might be coming up. It all adds to the experience. This is college. You're not supposed to be living in a nice looking place.

Community Bathrooms

The best thing about community bathrooms is that you don't have to clean them. With that said, a lot of people treat them like they don't have to clean them. So, be considerate. A lot of people live there besides you. Guys: don't pee on the seat. (A good rule of thumb is to always leave it up when it's not being used.) Girls: don't leave used tampons on the floor. You probably just made a weird face, but you would be mortified by some of the horror stories RAs will tell you. The way some people treat bathrooms is downright offensive. Always wear foot protection. Buy a pair of cheap flip-flops to wear in the shower. It's not advised to ever walk around in the bathroom barefooted; and never, ever go in there only wearing socks. That's just gross. The good news is that every few days, a nice man or woman will spray the whole thing down with bleach. This will kill every living thing in the room, and the counters and floors will probably be clean enough to eat off (although I don't recommend it). But don't worry; Larry from down the hall will come back drunk later and pee all over the wall. Awesome. Honestly, community bathrooms aren't as bad as they're made out to be. Most people actually take care of them; it's just the few jerks that ruin it for everyone else. Don't let it be you. Oh, and did I mention that you don't have to clean them?

Open Your Door

If you're just sitting in your room hanging out, leave your door open. It tells other people to stop by and say hey. An open door lets other residents know you're available to go play Frisbee, watch a movie, get something to eat, or millions of other things. It's a way to be sociable without actually leaving your room. But close it when you're trying to study. Having it open invites others in to hang out. There are enough distractions in your room already; you don't need people stopping by to see what's up to add fuel to your procrastination.

Lock Your Door

When you leave the room, lock the door. I know how obvious that sounds, but it's amazing how many iPods, DVDs, and laptops end up missing because a person didn't lock his door. If you're just going to the bathroom, you're probably safe. If you're going to take a shower, lock the door. But *do not forget the key*. Unless you just enjoy walking down to the front desk in nothing but a towel, remember to take the key with you. Most dorms keep track of how many times you get locked out, and after a certain number, they charge you for a lock change. So don't get robbed, and don't lose money because you were forgetful.

The Ultimate Crime

This is the most important paragraph in this chapter. (If you get nothing out of the rest of this section, take heed of this.) Living in the dorm comes with a lot of rules. However, none is greater than the cardinal rule of dorm life: *do not burn popcorn at 3:00 AM*. There is no better advice I can give you. If you burn popcorn, or anything else for that matter, you're likely to set off the fire alarm. Now, at home, it's not that big a deal. You just open a window and wave away the smoke until the alarm stops beeping. But in the dorm, it's a little different. If the alarm goes off, the fire department is *required* to come check on it, and everyone else in the building is *required* to evacuate. So at 3:00 AM., when most people are asleep, you will become a very hated individual. And they'll all know it was you. Someone saw you coming out of the smoke-filled kitchen, and it won't take long for everyone in the dorm to find out who's responsible for their late night excursion to the parking lot. When it comes to burnt popcorn, just say no.

Laundry

It's time to do your own laundry. It's really not that hard, I promise. (If you have absolutely no clue, turn to chapter 11.) There are two main rules for washing clothes in the dorm. 1. Always make sure you have enough quarters. The change machine only breaks when it's time for *you* to do laundry, so plan ahead. 2. Don't leave your clothes in the dryer unattended for too long. People have been known to steal them, underwear and all. And when people need to use the dryer after you, they tend to just put your clothes on the floor. Great. So set an alarm on your phone so you'll know when to go get your clothes out, especially if you wear expensive jeans.

Storage

Storage is a necessity that is hard to come by, and your room is not going to be able to fit all the crap that you want to put in it. So you're going to *have* to find a way to make extra space. Buy some bed lifts to raise your bed up higher. You'd be surprised how much storage space is created from lifting a bed eight inches. Bunking the beds is a really good idea to create more space, as well. It should give you enough room to bring in a couch and coffee table. Those tall plastic stackable drawers are also a great way to create storage and stay organized.

Moving Out

You will probably gather a good amount of crap as the year progresses. For some reason, stuff just tends to collect in the crevices of dorm rooms, and by May, you start wondering where it all came from. Just remember, everything you put in has to come out. And you don't want to be the guy all the RAs are waiting on to leave. Trust me, they won't treat you very nicely. To avoid being called really terrible names, pack up early. Go through all your stuff before finals roll around. Donate what you don't want or need anymore. Throw away all the randomly accumulated trash. Be ready to leave **before** you have to be. If you make trips home late in the year, take stuff with you. Life gets a lot more convenient if you can fit everything in your car on move-out day and only have to make one trip. If you live a long distance away, consider renting a small storage unit for the summer. It's cheap and can save you a lot of hassle; plus, there's probably someone still hanging around the dorm who will help you move it all.

Moving Off Campus

Living off campus can be extremely isolating. Make sure you have a large enough social network to not be left on the island alone. Reminders for on-campus events and activities will no longer be shoved in your face on a daily basis. Spontaneous ideas to watch a movie or go play basketball will be replaced by drawn out text conversations and planning. Now, there's absolutely nothing wrong with moving off campus. It's another adventure wrought with its own challenges and triumphs. But there are a lot of differences from the dorm. You have to worry about bills, leases, landlords, and commuting, to name a few. (You also have to clean the bathrooms.) But if you and a bunch of friends want to get a house together, then go for it. It's a totally different experience that will hopefully better prepare you for living in the real world. Just know what you're getting into before you make the transition.

7: Partying

Let's just be honest: partying is a big part of college. It should never be *the* big part of college, but you should definitely get out of your room and have some fun. From keggers to LAN (local area network) parties, there's probably something going on around town to help you unwind after grinding through another week. The trick is being able to balance that fun with class. If you can effectively manage what you do socially with what you do academically, not only will you graduate, but you will also build relationships with people that will help you down the road. But, you have to be smart about it. Partying requires a fair amount of common sense. Don't leave home without it.

The Number One Rule

Here's the number one rule of partying: ***when in doubt, get out.***
If you're unsure about the place, the people, or what's going on,
then leave. There will be more parties; I promise. Having an uneasy
feeling is usually your intuition trying to tell you something. Listen
to that feeling. If you see somebody with a gun or doing something
obviously illegal, it's a good idea to roll out. The wrong people get
shot or go to jail on a daily basis. Don't be one of them.

Study Before You Party

If you're going to party at night, study during the day. Not only
will it help your grades, but you will also have a better time while
you're out if you're not worried about that upcoming midterm.
However, don't party ***the night before*** a test. Even if you do study
during the day, staying up too late, not eating right, and drinking
will seriously inhibit your brain function when you're trying to
recall the information. So make sure there's enough recovery time
between the party and the test.

Know Your Limits

You need to know when it's time to cut yourself off. Alcohol
poisoning is a very big deal; people die from it. Drinking can
be a great way to have a good time. Overdrinking can be a great
way to wind up in the emergency room. The phrase "holding
your liquor" is just another way to say, "I'm going to need a new
liver soon." Your system can handle a certain amount of alcohol
without much trouble. But if you drink too much, you can cause
your internal organs some serious damage.

Have a Plan

Know where you're going to go and what you're going to do **before** you go out. Make sure people know where you'll be in case something happens, and figure out how you're getting home. Make sure you know the cab company's number and that you have enough cash to pay for one. Developing a plan beforehand is a lot easier than trying to figure things out on the fly, especially if you've been drinking.

Don't Go Alone

Always go with a friend who you know you can trust. Don't go with someone who will ditch you halfway through the night. If you're going to drink, have a friend that will be able to take you home. Getting into a car with someone you don't know is just as bad an idea now as it was when you were eight years old. Don't do it. And don't be the friend who runs off. If you came with people, leave with them.

Eat Before You Go

Drinking with nothing in your stomach is a quick way to end the night early. If you haven't eaten in a while, you're likely to drink more than you normally would, get drunker than you normally would, and get sicker than you normally would. Not eating before you go out is another factor that leads to a nasty hangover, so fill up before you leave the house. Also, food at bars can be expensive and is rarely worth the price.

Stay Hydrated

Alcohol is a diuretic. The more you drink, the more your body is encouraged to get rid of its water. This is partially where hangovers come from, so make sure you drink plenty of water before you go and even more while you're out. (It's usually free, so you've really got no excuse not to.) Don't drink soft drinks instead. They are also diuretics and will cause you to become even more dehydrated. And even if you're not drinking, partying in general just takes it out of you. Whether you're dancing or sitting around playing video games and drinking soda, your body is losing water. So, keep it full of H_2O. You'll wake up feeling a lot better.

New People

Parties are great for meeting new people and setting up social networks. You could get to know someone at a random frat party who helps you get a job two years later. However, it's really hard to get to know other people when you're throwing up off the balcony, so don't get so drunk that you can't interact with people. You might be missing prime opportunities. Also remember that there are a *lot* of creepers out there. Be wary of them. Never trust a drink you didn't see poured, and never think someone is "too nice" to mean you harm. I'm not telling you to run from people you don't know, and by all means, talk to strangers. It's how you meet new people, after all. But not all of them have good intentions. Here's another place where having a good friend with you helps. Make sure that friend won't let you do something stupid like leave the party with the thirty-year-old you just met. Just use common sense.

The Money

Partying can be expensive. Paying to get in clubs, buying a new outfit to go out in, and cab fare can get a little ridiculous. Oh, and by the way, alcohol will decimate a bank account. It's really not that hard to spend a hundred dollars at a bar. To avoid it, don't open a tab. Pay for each drink as you order it. If your drinks are just being added to a credit or debit card, it's hard to judge just how much money you're spending. Bars know that people will buy alcohol no matter what, so they don't mind charging stupid prices. However, a lot of bars will offer deals on certain nights or at particular times, so it is possible to save some money while you're out.

Party Tricks

You should learn one really cool party trick that doesn't involve bodily harm, get really good at it, and then use it a few times per year. Don't do it too often; it'll lose its luster. Go online and find tricks using playing cards, quarters, napkins, or anything else you would find readily available at a party. It's a great icebreaker and can help you meet new people. And never show anyone how you do it; that totally destroys the spark.

Passing Out

First of all, passing out is just really uncool. It annoys the people around you and bothers whoever owns the house you're at. And your friends probably don't enjoy having to carry you. It also sets you up for some serious embarrassment; and trust me, the Facebook pictures will not be kind. So if you're going to pass out, make sure it's on purpose. ***Always take your shoes off.*** Having your shoes off tells everyone else that you meant to fall asleep where you did. It's also the universal law that if your shoes are off, no one should mess with you. Not everyone abides by this law, but for the most part, it stays true across the board. If you're found with your shoes on, be prepared to have inappropriate words and drawings on your face, usually written in permanent marker. You should also not be surprised if your lifeless body is placed in compromising positions and then taken pictures of. College kids are mean, so don't get caught passed out with your shoes on.

Don't Overstay

Know when the party's over. Don't hang around until you're the last one there and everyone else is trying to go to sleep. It's a good way to not get invited back. If you're bad at realizing when it's time to go, ask a friend to tell you. Ask him to split the cab fare home. Some people will tell you to just sleep on their couch, but if they don't invite you, then don't assume it's cool. Just go home. (Unless the sun's up. Then you should consider going to Waffle House.)

Dancing Like a Slut

Here's the deal: dancing like a slut makes you a slut. Period. If you looked like a whore on the dance floor, a guy is going to assume you're a whore when he talks to you. I realize how harsh that is. But that's just the way it is. If you move like a hoochie-mama, men are going to treat you like one. So, by all means, dance; but don't dance in a way that suggests guys can take advantage of you.

Underage Drinking

Here's a fun fact: underage drinking is illegal. Now, if you really want to drink, then you're gonna drink. There's nothing anybody can say to stop you. But if you do it, you give up all rights to whining about getting caught, arrested, and having to pay a huge fine. (Plus, you get to have your parents lecture you. Awesome.)

"I Was Drunk"

You've probably heard the excuse "I was drunk" a billion times. And it can even be the beginning of a pretty funny story. But it does not work when the police are involved. If you get arrested and charged with a crime, "I was drunk" is only going to work in your head. No police officer, judge, or jury will have pity on you because you were intoxicated. If anything, they'll treat you worse. So don't be stupid. Don't allow alcohol to get you expelled from school or arrested. I know it seems farfetched, but it happens every single semester. According to the odds, you'll probably even know someone it happens to. Most crimes committed on college campuses involve alcohol. Don't let it happen to you.

Drunk Driving

Bob Simon of 60 Minutes[4] reported that drunk driving kills more than thirteen thousand Americans per year—that's one every thirty-nine minutes. And ironically, the drunk driver usually survives. Now, I didn't write this book to lecture people, but nobody should have any sympathy for anyone who chooses to get behind the wheel after drinking. And forget about getting a DUI, going to jail, losing your scholarship, and throwing away job opportunities. We're talking about ripping apart other people's lives—and not just the victims' lives. Think about what your parents would have to go through the next day at work after it's been in the paper that you *killed* someone while drunk driving. Think about how for the rest of your life, you will have to deal with the fact that you're still here while someone else isn't, and *it's your fault.* There's no reconciling that. There's only learning to live with it. And there's absolutely no excuse for it. There is a friend in your phone who will come to pick you up. There is a cab driver who will gladly come by and get you. There is a couch you can sleep on. There are just way too many reasons to not drive drunk, and other people stand to lose too much if you take the risk. (I'll get off my soapbox now.)

Naked Pictures
Don't take naked pictures of yourself. *Ever.* For any reason. Period. It might seem like a good idea at the time, and the notion might be sexy in your mind, but way too many things can go wrong. It's definitely not worth the risk of everyone, including your mother, seeing them. And the pictures inevitably come out. Maybe because you broke up and now she's mad, so she sends the picture of you in nothing but a cowboy hat to everyone she knows. Or maybe your friend goes through your phone without asking and then decides it would be funny if all your other friends saw your girlfriend naked. Or maybe your phone gets stolen and the thief thinks it would be great to sell those pictures to a porn site. (It really does happen.) The fact is that there is way too much at stake to even chance it. If you want someone to see you naked, don't send him a picture.

A Few Random Facts about Alcohol[5]
(If You're Gonna Drink, Know the Facts)

o   1 in 5 college students doesn't drink at all.

o 300,000 of today's college students will eventually die of alcohol-related causes.

o 159,000 of today's first-year students will drop out next year for alcohol or drug related reasons.

o The average student spends about $900 per year on alcohol.

o The average student spends about $450 per year on books.

o One night of heavy drinking has been found to impair thinking for up to 30 days.

o Birth control increases intoxication.

o A woman gets drunk faster during the days right before her period.

o Alcohol increases estrogen levels in men. Chronic alcoholism has been associated with loss of body hair and muscle mass and the development of swollen breasts, shrunken testicles, and impotence.

8: COMPUTERS

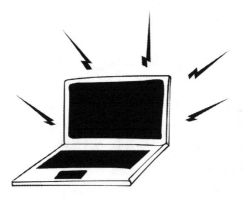

Computers have taken over college campuses. Nearly every class will require you to use one, and it's doubtful you'll go a day without logging on. So the better you are with them, the better your life's going to be. They can be extremely complex, but you don't have to be a programmer to understand the main components. Knowing just a few simple things will save you both time and money and will keep you from losing a twelve-page paper at two o'clock in the morning.

Desktop or Laptop

Honestly, it doesn't matter. Laptops are more portable. Desktops are cheaper. They both get the job done. If you already have one, don't go out and buy the other. You can type papers, send e-mails, and surf the Internet effectively on either one, so there's not some huge advantage in having one or the other. However, some majors might require you to bring a laptop to class, so check with the department head to find out if your department has any specific computing needs. If you *are* going to buy a new computer, weigh all of your options first. A laptop is usually more expensive, but it's a lot easier to move. And if your campus has wireless Internet, a laptop allows you to get out of your room and work on papers outside. A desktop is usually cheaper, easier to upgrade, and easier to fix, but you won't be able to take it to the coffee shop or library without some serious inconvenience. Whichever way you decide to go, make sure to ask the seller if the store offers a discount for students. A lot of them do, and it could save you some money.

Laptops and Class

Unless it's specifically required, ***do not*** take a laptop to class. (Many professors don't allow them anyway.) It's cumbersome, it could get stolen, it's at greater risk of being damaged, and, most importantly, you're going to spend most of your time on Facebook. (The sound of typing can also be really annoying to the people around you.) Typing your notes seems like a cool thing to do, but you can actually take better notes if you write them. Pen and paper offers a lot more freedom to draw pictures and charts, and it's a lot easier to make personal notes in the margins. Most classrooms don't have available plugs, either, which makes battery life an issue. Did I mention that pen and paper don't run out of power and lose your work?

Buying Software

Don't buy *anything* until you're sure you can't get it for free. Universities offer a lot of different programs, from anti-viruses to video editing software, for free. Before you buy anything, check with the university to see what they offer. (Some of it might not be listed on the Web site, so ask around.) And anything they don't give away for free, you can probably get at a discount just for being a student. The Internet is the land of the student deal, where companies offer awesome discounts if you're enrolled in school. All you have to do is search for these discounts. There are a bunch of great Web sites out there; there are a lot of scams, too, though, so be careful.

Anti-Virus Software

Most schools require you to have an anti-virus program, but even if yours doesn't, you definitely need to get one. Your college might offer a free one through its Web site, or you might need to download one from the Internet, but the biggest thing is this: *don't pay for it*. There are way too many free programs that work too well to be paying for one. Ask an IT person or a computer major what the best free program is right now. Trust me, they'll know. And make sure you install it before you get on campus. The last thing you want is to hook up to the network and get a virus on the first day.

Back Up Periodically

Computers tend to crash and die at very inopportune times. Make sure you back up your files, so you don't lose everything. Burn important data onto a CD or DVD or put it on an external hard drive. Hopefully, your system will never crash or get stolen, but if it does, you won't lose an entire semester's worth of work. Your operating system should even have a backup program built into its system tools with easy to follow steps. There are also numerous online backup sites that act as Internet storage sheds for a monthly fee. The biggest thing to remember is not to wait until it's five minutes too late to think about backing up your files.

Viruses

Viruses happen. Even if you have a great anti-virus program, some bugs can still get in. So, if you receive an e-mail, Facebook message, or file that looks suspicious, **_don't open it_**. The best way to avoid viruses is responsible Web browsing, so don't download anything you don't know is safe. (This includes porn.) And if you all of a sudden get a message from a person you never talk to, it's probably a virus. If you do happen to open a file and suspect it's messing with your computer, don't panic. It can be fixed. Run your anti-virus software and do a scan of your whole system. Hopefully, it will find the problem and fix it.

If your computer catches a really nasty bug and you use a Windows machine, try to use **_system restore_**, which is located under _system tools_ in the accessories of the start menu. If you are unable to restore, use a friend's computer to search for a possible fix. If all of your files are backed up, and you have the operating system's original install/recovery disk, you can reinstall the system to fix the problem. If you haven't backed up recently and can't afford to lose the files, consult the computer wizard down the hall or go to the university's computer repair center. It'll probably cost some money, but it's better than not having your files or use of your computer.

More Safeguards

- o When working on a paper or presentation, save after every paragraph. This way, if the power happens to go out or your system just decides to restart itself, you won't lose any significant amount of work.
- o When finished with a paper, project, or presentation, e-mail it to yourself. This ensures nothing will happen to it and allows you to access the file from anywhere with an Internet connection.
- o Never leave your jump drive, backup CD or DVD, or external hard drive with your laptop. They'll both be stolen.
- o Run a virus scan on your computer at least once per week.
- o Don't leave your laptop on the couch. Your roommate will sit on it.

Homepage

Make the university's Web site your homepage. It'll help you avoid missing out on upcoming dates and events. They usually put reminders about scheduling times and future programs on campus. The site will also tell you when class has been canceled due to snow, hurricanes, or zombie outbreaks. You're probably going to be using the site a great deal anyway; you may as well start there every time.

Alternative E-mail

Set up an alternative e-mail address. This can help you be more organized and will probably have a larger storage capacity than your university e-mail. It's a good idea to use the college's address strictly for school related e-mails and to use a different e-mail address for personal and business use. (The second address is especially useful for receiving large files.) It's also helpful to have your own personal account that isn't connected to the school when applying for jobs. Just make sure the address isn't something like sexy_gurl207. Employers take note of such things, and believe it or not, a silly or inappropriate e-mail address could keep you from getting a job.

Academic Forums

Nearly all universities use some sort of online system for classes. Your school might call it Blackboard, or eCollege or something else; whatever the name, it's just another way for professors to assign you work. The system will usually have a forum, but it's not your typical Web site forum. You can't make stupid or offensive comments and then hide behind a username. No matter what you say, the entire class will know it was you, so think before you type.

Some of these academic forums have been known to have a glitch or two, and they don't mind freezing. Normally, when a Web site freezes, you can just click refresh and the problem fixes itself. However, with these forums, clicking refresh will erase anything in an open text box. That means the last hour you spent typing that incredibly thought-provoking post will be about as productive as playing Farmville on Facebook. Don't be a victim. Type out everything in a word processor, and then copy and paste it onto the forum. Most forums also don't have spelling or grammar check, which can make you look a little ignorant when your post has a bunch of misspelled wrods.

Identity Theft

Identity theft has become a huge problem, so keep all of your passwords and ID numbers safe. Be wary of who asks for your personal information, and always make sure the site is secure before you type in any credit card numbers or any other private information. When you buy stuff online, make sure each site is credible. If you're not sure, it's better to go somewhere else than to risk someone draining your bank account. Also check your credit report on a regular basis. The three main bureaus are required by law to send you one per year at no charge; all you have to do is request this. (Any company charging for a credit report is probably a scam.) Your bank may also provide a credit monitoring service, which will update you anytime your report changes. People can hijack your Facebook or e-mail accounts as well, so use a password that can't just be guessed. Use numbers and capital letters to make your password really strong. Also, be aware of giving out your e-mail address. Spam can quickly max out your inbox space. (And please don't keep your passwords on post-it notes next to your computer or in a file labeled "passwords.")

Stealing Music

Most campuses have network restrictions set up to keep you from stealing or sharing files via torrents. There are ways to get around the restrictions, but it's highly unadvised. If you get caught, your Internet access can be taken away, you can be suspended, and you might even experience legal consequences. If you live off campus, it's still a pretty bad idea to steal or share files via torrents. The companies that own the rights to the files monitor illegal downloading and will contact your Internet service provider (ISP) to request your information. If you're lucky, the ISP will send a cease and desist letter to the person who pays the bill. The letter will also list all the files that you have downloaded illegally, so good luck explaining to your mom why you downloaded the entire collection of Girls Gone Wild. If you continue to download files, you could be taken to court. (Some ISPs won't even send a letter. They'll just rat you out.)

Porn

Just like having sex with multiple partners, looking at porn greatly increases your computer's chance of getting a virus. Porn sites are notorious for infecting systems with viruses, spy ware, and Trojans, and the more sites you go to, the more likely you are to cripple your computer. And because the sites secretly download files to your hard drive, looking at a lot of porn can cause your whole system to run slower. (You've been warned.)

Fun fact: When Internet porn became popular, the number of sexual assaults went down. Now, isn't that a good thing? Not exactly. Sure, the lowering of assaults is awesome, but another problem arose. Men were becoming less attracted to real women. Porn was creating a fantasy world that real life didn't live up to. Just so we're clear: "porn stars" are actors paid to *act*, that pizza delivery job in the video isn't as glamorous as they suggest, and watching too much porn really can ruin your relationships with real people.

Common Words Defined

Facebook is a networking site where possible employers can find out what kind of person you are; having pictures of yourself getting wasted or having your interests include "getting high" probably won't help you get hired.

A *firewall* is security software or hardware that can actively block unauthorized users from gaining access to your computer. A firewall may also act to prevent you from accessing unauthorized content.

A *flash or thumb drive* is a small electronic device, more portable than a hard drive, used to temporarily store digital data.

Spam is unsolicited e-mail, often advertisements, sent out over a computer network to many addresses, usually indiscriminately.

Spyware refers to programs that secretly monitor and report the actions of a computer user.

Sharing files via *torrents* is a method of peer-to-peer file sharing that relies on each user having a piece of the file to be downloaded and sharing those pieces among each other until everyone has the complete download.

A *Trojan* is a piece of software that appears to perform or actually performs a desired task for a user while performing a harmful task without the user's knowledge or consent.

A *virus* is a program that can be transmitted between computers via networks (especially the Internet) or removable storage devices, such as CDs, DVDs, USB drives, etc., generally without the knowledge or consent of the recipient.

9: CLASS

College would be the perfect way to live if it weren't for class. With that said, class is the reason you're here. It's why you're spending thousands of dollars on tuition. (Or at least *someone's* paying thousands of dollars.) And here's the deal, class is the means to the end. Class gets you the diploma, which gets you the job, which gets you the paycheck, which gets you the food. (Let's be honest; we all really just want to eat good food when you get right down to it.) Understanding how class works is one of the most important things you need to learn. It'll help you graduate faster, and it might even help you get a good job. (Which will lead to good food.)

GO

This is probably the most commonsense paragraph in the whole book. *Go to class.* Yeah, I know; that idea is groundbreaking—revolutionary, even. But not going to class is the main reason it takes a lot of people six years to graduate, and it's why many never graduate at all. You have to get good at going when you don't want to. Even when you wake up feeling like garbage, you need to roll out of bed and fight your way to class. Just because there are no immediate consequences doesn't mean skipping won't screw you in the end. Even if there's no attendance policy, professors take note of who's there and who isn't. And don't expect them to help you out when final grades roll around if you haven't been going to class. Professors have been known to bump grades up for people who put forth effort, so even if you fail every test, the professor might help you out if she knows you've been to every class. They just want to know you care, and the best way to prove it to them is to show up. No excuses. Bite the bullet. Even if you didn't finish the term paper, even if you feel like crap, and even if it's the bane of your existence, it's time to grow up. Class is why you're paying thousands of dollars to be here, after all, and professors get paid regardless. (Plus, going every day makes not showing up because of sickness a lot more credible.)

Read the Syllabus

Everything you need to know is on the syllabus, so read it. Tests, due dates, homework, books to buy, office hours, expectations—the list goes on and on. Everything the professor wants you to know is on there. (Granted, it's all subject to change, but changes tend to be few and far between.) Professors like to have everything planned and scheduled out; it helps them, as much as it helps you, to stay organized. Read it carefully. Your teacher won't mind taking points off your paper because it's in the wrong format, and he might not say anything about it in class. As soon as you get it, mark all the important dates on a calendar. Don't bomb a test because you forgot when it was.

Easy Classes

Don't make easy classes difficult. Go to class. Do the work. Get the A. Way too many people get a B or a C in simple classes because they don't show up, and they don't turn in the assignments. Easy classes are designed to boost your GPA; don't let laziness screw things up. And please, please do not fail an easy class. It will hurt for a long time. Every time you think about your GPA, you'll cringe remembering the easy A's you let slip away for no reason.

Majors

As J. R. R. Tolkien wrote, "Not all who wander are lost." But the more you wander between majors, the more money you lose. Changing majors can seriously add time to your stay here. It's important to find the right one, but it gets to a point when it's more important to get out of here. The majority of college graduates don't even go into their major's field anyway. So when someone asks what you are going to do with your degree, tell them anything you want. Don't stress too much about it. Find something you enjoy, and then work hard at it. It's not about knowing what you want to do. (The most interesting old people in the world still don't know what they want to do.) College is about getting a degree. What discipline it's in is really not that important.

The Library

Get familiar with the library. You may have to visit it often for different classes. Tours and instructional sessions are usually offered during the first couple of weeks of school; take advantage of them. Learning to use the library will save you a ton of time and make writing papers a whole lot easier. And when you're writing a paper or doing research, talk to the people at the help desk. They have the answers to pretty much everything and will be extremely excited to share them with you. Don't spend all day hunting down a book when someone can direct you to it in thirty seconds.

Cancelled Class

A cancelled class tells you that God exists and He loves you very much. There are fewer things that will make you feel better about a day. Go do something productive. (Or don't, the choice is yours.)

The College Cycle

Nearly everything in college moves in cycles. You'll go weeks without having hardly anything to do and then have a test in every class and four papers due over a three-day period. Here's how you beat it: *prepare during the calms to dominate during the storms.* When you're experiencing a lull, consult your syllabi. They will tell you everything coming up and will warn you of the impending onslaught of work. Use the down time to get started early. Go ahead and start researching for that paper and studying for that test. It will seriously lighten your load during the hell weeks. While your classmates are totally stressed out, you'll be able to relax and treat all those backbreaker days as, well, just regular days.

Papers

Start Early
Don't wait until the night before your paper's due to get started. Your professor can tell the difference between a paper with substance and a paper full of BS, so start at least a few days ahead of time; putting it off until the last minute can be detrimental to your sleep cycle and your stress level and will usually lead to a lower grade.

Wikipedia
Wikipedia is not a credible source. However, it is a great place to get ideas. (Professors have been known to post false information on the site just for fun.)

Speak the Language
Know the lingo. Use the key words of the course. (It also helps if you use them correctly.) Professors tend to repeat the same important words; use them. It shows you've been paying attention and that you understand the material.

Plagiarism
Plagiarism has a very low success rate nowadays. If you found it on the Internet, so will your professor. I mean, these are extremely smart people we're dealing with here. They realize when the work's not yours, and there are all sorts of programs they can load your paper into that will show exactly where you got your information. So please, don't insult their intelligence. They won't appreciate it, and the consequences are severe. If you didn't get the paper done, take the late penalty. Copying and pasting a paper from an online source will fail you and possibly even expel you. This isn't high

school. Professors don't play around, and they take plagiarism personally.

Make sure to cite all sources **_properly_**. Don't be unintentionally guilty of plagiarism, as unintentional plagiarism will fail you, too. Bibliography Web sites such as EasyBib.com will make your life a lot easier and can keep you from screwing up your bibliography. Find a site you like and bookmark it.

Ask for Help

Your school probably has a writing center designed to help students with papers. It's full of people who are both good at writing papers and willing to assist you. You should go meet them. You should become friends.

Don't Shortchange

Either your paper has substance or it doesn't; don't try to shortchange your professor. Don't go screwing with the font or spacing just so you can meet the minimum requirements. And if the assignment says five pages, don't try to get away with four and a half. Five pages is five pages. Professors aren't stupid; they see when you've messed with the format to increase the length. They can tell by how long it took to read. Such things might even offend them. Don't be surprised if you lose points.

Notes

What's Best for You

Develop your own personal note taking system. There are so many different ways to take notes; it's ridiculous. If you Google "note taking," you get 1.8 million results. You just have to do what's best for you. Are you better with pictures? Do you remember acronyms better? Whatever the case may be, figure out what's best, and then stick to it.

Double Up
If the lecture notes are online, print them off before class and take notes on them during the lecture.

Be Concise
Don't write down everything the professor says; be concise. Pick out the key points and put them down in your own words. Develop a system of abbreviations to speed up the process. Make a legend to remember them all if you have to.

Keep Good Records
Date your notes in order to keep good records. It will help you stay organized and will make them easier to refer back to when you're studying.

The Golden Rule
If it's on the board, it goes in your notes. If it's important enough for your professor to write down, it's probably going to be on the test.

Tests

Points
Points are usually hard to come by. You might only have two tests for the entire class, so make good on your opportunities. Screwing up on one test might be all it takes to destroy your grade for the

whole class. And if you do completely blow a test, ask for extra credit possibilities. A lot of professors won't give them to you, but if one does, make good on it. Blowing off extra credit tells the professor you don't care, which means she won't mind failing you.

Before the Exam

Talk to the professor before the test to make sure you're studying the right material. He might not give you much, but anything at all helps. Just don't go in there without knowing any of the material. Show him you've studied a little bit. He'll be more likely to help you if he thinks you've already been putting forth effort.

Really Know It

Don't just memorize the information; really know it and actually understand the concepts. Learn the material in a way that you would be able to teach it to someone else. Knowing how everything connects is how you graduate with honors.

Studying

Designate a specific place to study. Wire your brain so that it knows that when you go to that certain spot, it's time to focus and retain information. Again, **never study in bed**.

Cheating

I'll be honest with you; it's not hard to cheat. Class sizes are often big, especially in large universities, seats are close together, and professors don't always pay the closest of attention. If you really want to look on someone else's paper, you'll probably get the chance to do so. But here's the deal. Over the next few years, you're going to have a ton of opportunities to sell out. Situations you can't even imagine are going to cross your path, and you're going to have to make tough decisions about which way you want your life to go. Don't sell out over something as small as an algebra test. (Or any test for that matter.) It's just not worth it. And we're not even talking about failing the class if you get caught. We're dealing with who you are as a person. I realize it doesn't seem like that big of a deal, but keep in mind that people rarely crumble in a day. It's usually a slow fade.

Scheduling

Two Strategies

1. **Time**. If you're better at certain times of the day, you may want to schedule your classes during those times. If you struggle to get up at 8:00 AM, don't sign up for early morning classes. If you get the "itis" right after lunch, don't sign up for early afternoon classes. (The "itis" is that feeling of sluggishness and contentment one feels after eating a large meal.) Many people also schedule their classes around a daily nap. However, using the time strategy means you won't always get the best professors, and a lot of classes only have one scheduling option.

2. **Professor**. Many would rather base their schedules on the professors instead of the times of day. This is an especially good idea if you find a professor you really like; I advise you to take every class you can with him. You might have to wake up at the butt crack of dawn or be on campus late in the evening, but the right

professor can make it worth it. If you're unsure about a professor, go online and see what people say about him. There are numerous Web sites that allow students to warn about or recommend classes and teachers. Also ask older people; they know things, too.

Schedule Early

Don't miss out on classes you need because you were lazy; schedule early and sign up as soon as you can. (That means figuring out which classes you need or want *before* the day of.)

Schedule Too Many

Sign up for more classes than you're going to take. It allows you to find out what the classes and professors are going to be like, and then you can drop the ones you don't like.

Use the Campus Map

Use your campus map when scheduling so that you don't schedule back-to-back classes on opposite ends of campus. Professors don't appreciate you walking in late, and they don't usually care how far you had to run.

Back-to-Back

Scheduling back-to-back classes makes you more likely to go and eliminates long periods of time in between classes for you to get distracted.

Start Slow
You've got enough to worry about and adjust to, so start slow. Don't start out in CHEM 4000. Ease into it. Get the hang of college before you throw yourself into the fire.

Don't Trust Titles
Some really great classes have really bland titles, and some really terrible classes have really great titles, so don't trust the titles alone. Find out what the class is really about. Sometimes the title doesn't even fit the course's content at all.

Hold Your Spot
If you want a popular class but don't get to schedule until late, have someone sign up for it and hold your spot for you. When it's your time to schedule, your friend drops the class, and you take her spot. It's genius.

Fall or Spring Only
Some classes are only offered during the fall or spring semester each year. Know which ones they are. Don't get behind because you thought you could take the class next semester.

English Classes
Know how much reading a class requires. Three ENG classes in one semester could swamp you. And remember, not all English classes are created equal. Some professors like assigning a ton of papers; some don't. Know what you're getting into **before** you sign up.

Math Classes

Don't wait to take math classes. If your major only requires one or two, take them as soon as possible. Math has a tendency to fade away over time, and you don't want everything you learned in high school to just slip away. (If your major requires a lot of math, then you need to start taking math classes yesterday.)

Foreign Languages

Don't put gaps between foreign language classes. Continue them ASAP. You forget enough over Christmas break; don't let an entire semester roll by while you forget the entire vocabulary.

Electives

Take electives for more than just an easy A. Electives give you opportunities to learn about subjects totally out of your major. So, sign up for a class about insects or electromagnetism. You might have to work a little harder, but you can learn some really awesome stuff.

Dropping

There's no shame in dropping a class. If after the first test you know you're going to fail, it might be best to quit while you're behind. It's better than ruining your GPA. Just be aware of how dropping the class will affect your status, insurance, and financial aid before you go through with it.

A Failed Class

Retake a failed class the very next semester. Don't let the information you actually understand fade away. And don't throw anything away before you retake the class; use all the tests and papers you didn't do well on to learn from your mistakes. So you failed a class; it happens. Just do what it takes to make it right.

Summer Classes
Take tough classes over the summer, when it's more laid back and you'll have more time to give. A summer class will also probably meet every day, which will keep the material fresh on your mind.

Community College
If there's a particular class you know you won't do well in, take it at a community college over the summer. It's cheaper, more relaxed, and you usually get more one-on-one attention.

Limit Your Course Load
One bad semester can crush a GPA. Limit the number of difficult classes you take in a semester so you can focus more time on each one.

The First Day

Plan Out Your Course
Know where you're going before the first day rolls around. Take your schedule and walk to all of your classrooms, finding the best way to get to each of them. It will save you time when classes actually start, and it will keep you from looking like a lost freshman.

Get There Early

College classes rarely have assigned seats, but people tend to sit in the exact same place every day. Getting there early not only looks good to the professor, but also insures you'll be able to get the seat you want.

The Best Seat

Figure out where it's best for you to sit. If you have trouble reading the board, sit in the front. If you have trouble paying attention, sit in the front. If you're weird about people being behind you, sit in the back. If you just really don't care, sit in the middle somewhere. It can make a big difference.

Identify What's Yours

Put your name and phone number on everything to identify what's yours. If a book, notebook, or calculator gets lost, you stand a much better chance of getting it back if it has a label. Not everyone wants to steal your stuff; some folks really do want to get it back to you.

The Wrong Class

If you find yourself stuck in the wrong classroom, and it's beyond the point of no return (i.e. the professor's already passing out the syllabus), don't make a big deal about it. Think of it as an opportunity to learn something unexpected. Just smile, take the syllabus, and find the right classroom later. To really have some fun, ask random questions about the course content. Who knows, you might find your major by wandering into the wrong class.

In Class

Be Prepared
Read and do assignments before the lecture. It will give you a better understanding, and you'll be ahead.

Raise Your Hand
Speak up and answer the questions you know. The professor will be less likely to call on you for the ones you don't know. Class will also move faster if people actually talk and don't just stare blankly when the professor asks a question. If you talk like you read the material, he'll be less likely to quiz you on it.

Other People
You don't have to agree with others, but you do have to respect them. Nothing will get you thrown out of class faster than ridiculing another student. This is college. Unprofessional behavior won't be tolerated. It's in all the syllabi; see for yourself.

Facebook
Become Facebook friends with some classmates. It's a great way to ask about classes you miss and to organize group projects. (Don't befriend the entire class; that's weird.)

Before a Break
Go to class the day before a break. Professors will often give quizzes or just hand out points for attendance.

10: Cell Phones

C ell phones have become a really big deal. It's a multi-billion dollar business, and there are only a handful of college students who don't have one. Cell phones have revolutionized the way we communicate with each other, but they have also created many new challenges and problems.

Paying for It

A cell phone can totally destroy a budget. Phones can cost hundreds of dollars, and the monthly bill can be equally expensive. But they don't have to be so costly. Inexpensive, quality phones can be purchased from stores like Wal-Mart. You won't be able to download a billion apps on these cheaper phones, but do you really need all those apps anyway? If you're unsure about being able to make a monthly payment, then just use pre-paid minutes. It's slightly more inconvenient, but it won't destroy your bank account, and you'll never go over on your minute limit. To save money on a monthly plan, you can turn off text messaging and Internet. It really is possible to have a phone for only a few bucks per month if you're willing to sacrifice.

Dependence

Many college students have become utterly dependent on their phones. To go a day without a phone would be worse than a day without food or water. It's really kinda sad. Cell phones have become an addiction. Without them, a person feels disconnected or like she's missing an appendage. Do yourself a favor. Leave the phone at home on purpose from time to time. Enjoy not being tied to it and having to glance at it every couple of minutes. It can be a truly freeing experience. And when you get back, remember that having missed calls lets you know people love you. (If you don't have any missed calls, I'm sure people still love you.)

Silent

Put your phone on silent while you're in class. Not on vibrate. Silent. A phone in your pocket, purse, or book bag can vibrate as loud as your ringtone plays. Some professors will kick you out if they hear it; some will answer the incoming call. Some even have policies of taking points off your final grade. So get in the habit of putting your phone on silent before you walk into class.

Texting

Texting destroys learning. It completely takes your mind off what is going on and disrupts your train of thought. If you really need to study, turn your phone off. If you're trying to study and have a conversation via text message, you're not going to absorb the material very efficiently. That means you'll have to study longer. Stopping to look at your phone every few minutes usually leads to reading the same information many times over.

Texting in Class

Just because your professor doesn't say anything doesn't mean he isn't taking note of the phone in your lap you keep glancing at. He's not stupid. He sees what you're doing, and he'll probably remember it when the time for final grades comes around. If you're texting, you're not paying attention. It's as simple as that. And in some lectures, all it takes is missing one key point to become totally lost.

Phone Safety

A new phone is expensive, so keep it safe. Don't carry it in your back pocket, as it'll only end up in the toilet. Way too many phones have been murdered by drowning. Put it in a protective case so it won't break when you drop it—and you're going to drop it. Don't put it on your nightstand above a glass of water. Many phones have been known to vibrate into suicide. Just treat it like a friend. If you don't think it's important to you, then try going two days without it. That'll show you just how much you really do rely on it.

Texting While Driving
Never, under any circumstances, text while driving. It can kill you and possibly other people, and it's already becoming illegal in a number of states. Whatever the message you need to read or send is, I promise it can wait. A text message about what time the party starts is definitely not worth veering off the road and winding up wrapped around a tree. Way too many people have already died because the message on a phone was more important than paying attention to the road. Don't be next.

Texting While Walking
Don't zone out while walking by texting at the same time. You tend to not pay attention where you're going, which is a good way to get hit by a person on a bicycle. Also avoid walking out in the road while texting, even if there's a crosswalk. Many people view those white lines only as a suggestion to stop, and getting hit by a car really ruins your day. You may legally have the right of way, but what good is the right of way when you can't feel your legs?

Seriously. Just stop. Send the text. Then start again. Over one thousand people were admitted to emergency rooms last year for injuries sustained when texting while walking. Some walked off curbs; some fell down steps; and some got hit by trucks. The point is that you need to stop focusing on that frivolous text conversation and realize where you're going.

11: How-To

There are a few things that you **really** need to know before you get out on your own. Some of these things might seem obvious to you, but I promise there are a lot of people who show up to college without a clue about how to do them.

Wash Clothes

This method is the most basic, efficient way to wash clothes. It will work the majority of the time, but if you have clothes that need to be washed in a specific way, then please follow the instructions on their tags.

1. Use the laundry detergent's measuring cup or cap to measure the detergent according to the product's instructions, and pour it into the washing machine. (Do not put dish soap in the washing machine. It will flood the entire area with bubbles and is a huge pain to clean up.)

2. Turn the water temperature to cold. This will keep colors from bleeding and fading and will keep your clothes from shrinking. However, any brand new dark fabrics should be washed separately to ensure they don't bleed onto lighter fabrics. Cold water also uses less power, which will save money on your power bill.

3. Start the washer before adding clothes. Adjust the water level to the size of your load.

4. Add your clothes. Close all zippers and empty all pockets as you put your clothes in the machine.

5. Close the lid.

6. When the washer is done, remove your clothes. Hang up any clothes that aren't supposed to go in the dryer.

7. Empty the dryer's lint tray.

8. Put your clothes into the dryer. Add a dryer sheet to help prevent static build-up.

9. Close the door, and select the appropriate drying temperature. Use low for delicates, medium for most fabrics, and high for cotton.

10. Turn the dryer on.

11. When the clothes are completely dry, remove and fold your clean laundry.

Jump-Start a Battery

Sometimes, you turn the key, and nothing happens. When this occurs, your battery is probably dead. It's a good idea to carry jumper cables in your vehicle, so when such a situation strikes, you won't be completely helpless. But you will need someone nice enough to let you borrow some juice.

1. Line up the two vehicles so the batteries are close enough to reach with the cables. Then, turn off the working car.

2. Open the hoods of both vehicles. Make sure both batteries are clear of corrosion. If you see corrosion, use water and paper towels to clean the batteries off. (To prevent corrosion in the future: with the vehicle off, coat the exposed clamps, posts, and wire with a thin layer of Vaseline.)

3. Start the vehicle with the good battery, and let it run for a minute. Connect one side of the positive jumper cable to the positive post on the dead battery and the other side

to the positive post on the good battery. Connect one end of the negative cable to the negative post of the good battery and the other end to an exposed piece of clean metal on the engine of the vehicle with the dead battery. (This decreases the likelihood of explosion.) Typically, the positive battery cable is red or orange. The negative (ground) cable is black. But double-check your jumper cables before you connect them to your vehicle. *Do not* touch the clamps together while they're connected to a battery.

4. Wait a couple of minutes for the battery to charge, and then attempt to start the vehicle. If it starts right up, remove the jumper cables in reverse order. Disconnect negative from the engine, negative from the good battery, positive from the good battery and positive from the previously dead battery.

5. Let your car run for a few minutes to charge the battery, and then switch the vehicle off. Now attempt to restart it. If the vehicle starts right up again, drive it for a while to make sure the battery is fully charged.

6. If it doesn't start, you will probably need a new battery. If you are close to an auto parts store, jump-start the car again, drive over, and purchase a new battery. If you're low on cash or just nowhere near a store, call a friend and get her to follow you home.

Change a Tire

You never know when you'll have a blowout in the middle of nowhere, so it's important to be able to fix it and get back on your way. Tires also tend to go flat in the rain for some reason, so the better you are at changing a tire, the sooner you can stop getting rained on. To be especially proficient at it, go out and practice from time to time. It won't take long, and it could save you a crap ton of time later.

1. Pull over to a safe area that is level and firm. Make sure you're a safe distance off the road.

2. Put the vehicle in park, engage the emergency brake, and turn on your hazard lights.

3. Locate your jack, tire iron, and spare tire.

4. If necessary, remove the hubcap from the flat tire.

5. Use the tire iron to loosen the lug nuts. Do not remove the nuts yet. Just loosen them to the point where you will be able to twist them off the rest of the way by hand.

6. Locate the place on the vehicle's frame where you can safely place the jack to elevate the car. If you're unsure, consult your vehicle's manual.

7. Elevate the vehicle so there is enough room to remove and replace the tire.

8. Remove the lug nuts.

9. Take the flat tire off, and replace it with the spare. (If your spare is a donut, do not exceed fifty-five miles per hour when you drive on it, and don't drive on it longer than you have to. It's not meant to be an everyday tire and will wear out rather quickly. Change it ASAP. Plus, what will you do when the doughnut goes flat?)

10. Tighten the lug nuts by hand. Make sure the tire is on evenly.

11. Release the jack to lower the car.

12. Tighten the lug nuts with the tire iron using a star pattern. The star pattern helps keep the tire balanced.

13. If necessary, replace the hubcap.

14. Place all tools and the flat tire back into your vehicle.

12: Important Dates

You'll find that your life will revolve around dates. Everything from moving in to paying bills to taking tests to submitting papers to moving out will depend on dates. So, managing a calendar becomes a very valuable skill. This chapter includes some of the most important dates for you to remember.

FAFSA

If you complete your FAFSA through the web application, it must be submitted by late June 30. Check the government's Web site each year for the specific date. Regardless, you should never wait that long. The longer you wait, the less money you get. Find out when your university's deadline for financial aid is. It could be quite different from the government's. Also find out if the deadline refers to the date and time of receipt or of your application's processing.

Scholarships

Scholarship deadlines are pretty rigid. Don't turn applications or paperwork in late and expect anyone to take pity on you. Get these forms done early so you can focus on other things. Scholarship deadlines can vary, so don't just assume they're all due at the same time. Don't leave money on the table because you didn't know the deadline.

Fees

Some classes require extra fees. Especially if you're taking a recreation class, be prepared to have to pay a little more to cover equipment, greens fees, etc. Don't forget to pay these fees, or you could get dropped from the class. A lot of clubs and organizations also require periodic fees. Write down due dates on your calendar. Don't blow your budget because you forgot about them.

Scheduling

Not knowing your scheduling date can lead to really crappy classes with really crappy professors next semester. Go ahead and shop around in advance for the classes you need and want; that way you can register for everything in a matter of minutes.

Add/Drop Classes

You usually have about a week to add a class once the semester starts and at least a few weeks when you can drop a course without a grade assignment. Dropping after the drop date will show up on your transcript, so put that date on your calendar.

Move In/Out

Don't show up too early; they might not let you in. Once your finals are over, go ahead and get packed up to leave. The RAs can't move out until everyone else in the building does, so if you take your time, you could make some enemies.

Midterms

Midterms will occur around the halfway mark in the semester. This is also usually the last day you can drop a class without a grade penalty (but check your school's policies to be sure). Remember, if you do really well on these, you'll be under less pressure when you take the finals. You never know how much gas you'll have left in the tank when the end of the semester rolls around, so study up.

Finals

Finals are rarely scheduled at the same time as when you normally have class. Professors have also been known to change the date. So once the date and time are confirmed, write them down and post the information in a highly visible location. Don't fail a final because you forgot to set your alarm for earlier, and don't wait until the last minute to figure these dates out. Your university probably already has the current semester's finals schedule posted on its Web site.

Parents' Birthdays

Send a card early for a parent's birthday so it gets there on time. Call your mom or dad in the morning so you don't wait around and forget. It doesn't have to be anything overly complicated. Just show you care; it'll go a long way. If you want to give them a really great gift, tell them about all the good grades you're making. (Don't lie.) They'll especially appreciate this if they had to take out a second mortgage to pay for tuition.

Other Birthdays

Here's another place where having a calendar is useful. Write down the birthdays of all close friends and close relatives. (Don't rely on Facebook to remind you of all the days you should remember.) When the day rolls around, call to show them you didn't forget. It's one of those small gestures that can mean a lot.

Mother's Day

Mother's Day is always the second Sunday in May. Don't forget it. It's just as important as her birthday. Again, send a card, and call her in the morning. Tell her you appreciate her. It's not hard to do and will mean more than you'll ever know.

Father's Day

Father's Day is always the third Sunday of June. This one deserves a card. But don't forget the phone call. If you want to have some fun, send him twenty bucks inside a goofy card that tells him to go buy something nice.

Bills

Not paying bills like tuition on time can be disastrous. Not only will the school drop you from your classes, but it will also take back your football tickets. Write down your due dates, and put them in a very visible place. Having your power, water, or cable shut off because you forgot to pay the bill really, really sucks. Plus, you'll usually have to pay an extra fee to get them turned back on.

Anniversaries

Remembering your parents' anniversary is not an absolute must, but it's still a good idea. They'll probably be somewhat surprised when you call home and wish them a happy day. (That surprise could help you later if you earn a D in Biology.) It doesn't have to be anything formal. Just let them know you care. ***Do not, under any circumstances, forget your own anniversary.*** It is better to die as a small child than to forget your anniversary and have to deal with the wrath of your girlfriend.

Valentine's Day

Valentine's Day is February 14, another day of infamy. It's a little harder to forget. Commercials and the holiday aisle at Wal-Mart will remind you on the first day of February, but men often wait until the last minute and then forget altogether. Don't be that guy. Order your flowers early.

Talk Like a Pirate Day

Every year, on September 19, you have the right, the privilege, even, to talk like a pirate all day long. So cast off ye inhibitions, and any scallywag who wants to scoff at ya can swab your poop deck. 'Tis only one day out the year a mate can speak as he pleases, so don't be a landlubber. (Fifteen men on a dead man's chest — Yo-ho-ho, and a bottle of rum.)

Cow Appreciation Day

Around the second week of July, Chick-fil-A celebrates Cow Appreciation Day. If you dress in partial cow attire, they'll give you a free entrée. If you dress in full cow garb from head to toe, they'll give you a free meal. So basically, you get free food for wearing black and white spots. That's not a bad deal.

One Day Without Shoes

Around the first of April, TOMS Shoes asks you to pledge to go barefoot for all or at least part of the day. It's a simple gesture that will give you a better understanding of what millions of children experience on a daily basis. Shoes are one of those small things we take for granted, and leaving them at home for a day can offer some stirring insight on the plight of other people around the world.

13. Strategies

*N*ow, you have all the information you need to conquer college. This chapter consists of some strategies others have used. I'm not saying they're what's best for you; they just work for these people. Think of them as samples to help you create your own set of strategies.

Before the First Day
Prepare yourself before classes ever start.

My strategy before the first day? That's simple. I print off my schedule and map out my path on campus. I ride a bike to class, so I look for good shortcuts and try to avoid high traffic areas. Then, I scope out bathrooms along my path to find the most unused ones. You just never know when you'll have to go.

Anthony, Senior

I set up my schedule to have a lunch break between one and two every day. By then, most of the regular lunch crowd is gone. Before the first day, I figure out the best places to eat that are close to my classes.

Matt, Junior

At first, I only buy the books I *know* I'll need. Professors change their minds sometimes, so I wait about buying books used later in the semester. Once they start assigning homework out of them, that's when I buy them.

Leigh, Senior

The First Day
It's critical to have a strategy for the first day of class.

I always show up early so I can get a seat against a wall. It also gives me a chance to meet some of the other people in the class. I've found a lot of girls show up early, too.

Neil, Junior

At the end of the first day, I organize a notebook for each class. I used to just throw everything into one notebook, but by the third week, I couldn't find anything whenever I needed it.

Brad, Senior

As soon as I get all the syllabi, I transfer the important stuff onto a calendar that hangs next to the door in my room. I may miss some assignments, but it's not going to be because I didn't know about them.

Lindsay, Junior

I don't buy books until after the first day. I usually drop at least one class a semester, and they rarely assign much homework on the first day anyway. Plus, now that I know a lot of people, there's usually someone in the class I can share a book with.

Pete, Senior

During my freshman year, I didn't meet anybody. My roommate was the only friend I really had. Thankfully, he got me involved with the on-campus events staff, and I got the chance to hang out with a lot of great people. My advice? Meet as many people as you can from the first day. Don't wait until you're a sophomore to venture out of your room. If I could go back and redo freshman year, I totally would.

Steve, Senior

Daily
A good strategy will get you through the everyday grind.

My mother always told me, "Don't be the smelly kid." I've got a friend whose roommate didn't wash his clothes the entire first semester. Obviously, their room smelled like butt. I carry a stick of deodorant in my bag just in case, especially in August when it's a thousand degrees outside.

Art, Senior

I set up a routine for every morning. As soon as I get up, I stretch for a few minutes and then do some pushups. It really gets the blood moving and helps wake me up. Then I check my e-mail while I eat a bowl of cereal. When professors cancel class, they usually don't send you an e-mail about it until seven AM.

Dave, Junior

Everyday, I make a to-do list. It helps me stay on top of things and not forget assignments. It also reminds me what time intramural games are.

Stacey, Junior

Before I leave every morning, I put some peanut butter crackers and fruit in my backpack. It tides me over until lunch and helps me get through 3 hours of lab.

Cassie, Senior

I got put on academic probation after my first semester. The classes weren't that hard; I just never went. Over Christmas break, my uncle offered me a job on his chicken farm. He said picking up dead chickens was a stable job with decent pay, and I wouldn't even need a college degree. I didn't miss a class that second semester. Now, I show up early and sit near the front. I ain't picking up dead chickens.

Blake, Junior

During my first year, I had a crappy job that I hated. So I checked bulletin boards constantly hoping something better would come along. Finally, it did. Now I get to drive a golf cart around campus and fix computers. You can call me a nerd if you want, but I'm not the one *walking* across campus.

Nathan, Senior

When scheduling, I base my class times on two things: lunch and an afternoon nap. It's funny how the nap is back in style once you get to college. I take one nearly every day. It gives me a boost of energy to finish out the day.

Cara, Senior

I work out four days a week. It's free and my school just opened up a new fitness center. I still use the old one though. Some people think it's too grimy, but the rust and cobwebs don't bother me much. It makes me feel like Clubber Lang from *Rocky III*.

Scotty, Junior

On some days, I have a two hour break between classes, so I've found a quiet lounge where I can study. I've learned that just reading back through my notes helps me remember a lot more information for the test. It's time I would normally be spending on Facebook anyway, so it's nice to actually get some productive work done.

Jena, Senior

I'm an English major, so I get stuck having to read a lot of crap I don't particularly care about. Anything in Old English just gets on my nerves. So I make it a point to read something every day that I actually enjoy. It might only be one chapter out of a book, but I'm reading *something* that's interesting.

Jim, Senior

During that first semester, I was afraid to get into deep conversations with people because I didn't want to say the wrong thing. Then I took some philosophy classes and realized no one's going to beat you up if you don't agree with them. Now, I make it a point to have at least one meaningful conversation every day. It can be about religion, politics, or quantum physics, just anything that actually matters.

Grant, Junior

I never pay more than five bucks for lunch. It took a little while, but now I've found all the places and all the meals I can get for five dollars or less. The best place? The Baptist Camus Ministry, hands down. A few sweet old ladies put together home cooked meals for about fifty of us and only charge three bucks a person. I'm Methodist, but no one seems to mind. It's not about religion; it's about enjoying good food.

Brian, Junior

I dated a guy during my second semester who seemed cool enough. It turns out he's one of those "my story is way better than your story guys." No matter what I said he knew someone who had done it better. Needless to say, that relationship only lasted a couple weeks. Now when anyone mentions him I tell them, "Oh, stay away from *that guy.*"

Holly, Senior

I had lived in the city my entire life. So when it came time to pick a college, I chose a school with tons of grass and lots of trees. It's kind of in the middle of nowhere, but I love it. I hang around outside all day long. I'm majoring in wildlife conservation which lets me be outside even more. College isn't about doing the same things you've done the last eighteen years; it's not an extension of high school. It's about exploring the unknown.

Dana, Junior

I go to at least one dorm sponsored program a week. Some of them are lame, but some turn out to be pretty good. So far I've learned how to make Korean food, played campus wide capture the flag, and discussed what I would do if zombies took over the world. Not a bad semester so far. They're a great way to meet new people and provide much needed breaks from studying.

Jarred, Junior

From my first day on campus I've been talking to the cafeteria staff. I ask them how their day is going. I compliment their earrings. I even invite them to eat with me when they go on break. And because I treat them right, they treat me right. They load my plate down with extra entrées and desserts. It's awesome. All people want is for you to be nice to them.

Patrick, Senior

Weekend

A weekend strategy is just as important as a daily one.

On the weekend, I make sure to get two things done: laundry and a phone call home. Every Sunday afternoon I update my parents on how everything's going. They really look forward to it, and considering how much money they're paying for me to be here, it's the least I can do.

Kelly, Junior

I hit up at least one party a month. I don't overdo it, but I have to have something to get me away from all the number crunching of engineering classes. A good Saturday night party helps me unwind and keep sane.

Chuck, Junior

During the week I'm lucky to get six hours of sleep a night. So on Saturday, I get at least nine. It helps me catch up on rest and gives me energy for the days ahead. By Monday, my body's ready to take on another week.

Jerry, Senior

On Sunday, I try to start on a paper. It might not be due for two or three weeks, but I go ahead and brainstorm, jot down notes, and make an outline. Then, when I sit down to type everything out, all my ideas are already in order. It saves a ton of time.

Crystal, Senior

I came to this school for one reason: the football. I go to every game including the away ones. I work my butt off during the week, but on Saturday, I'm not worrying about anything school related. Work hard, play hard, right.

Kevin, Junior

My friends and I constantly check the cheap movie bin at Wal-Mart for something we haven't seen. Every Saturday night we hang out in the dorm's lobby and watch a movie that either turns out to be really great or really terrible. Honestly, the worse the movie, the more fun we have.

Susan, Junior

During the last week of my first semester, my computer got a nasty virus. The whole system locked up, and I lost some pretty important files including the eight-page paper I had been working on. Now, every Sunday morning, I scan my computer for viruses and backup all my important data.

Cory, Senior

On Sunday night, I figure out everything I'm going to do for the week. I check each syllabus and the intramural schedule and decide how I'm going to spend my time. I like to be spontaneous on the weekends, but life goes a lot smoother during the week when you plan ahead.

Casey, Senior

Partying
A good strategy for partying is vital

I go to a lot of parties, but if I'm ever unsure about a situation, I get out quick. I'm not about to get shot, stabbed, or arrested.

If something's about to go down, I don't stick around to see the end of it.

Brent, Junior

Whenever I go out, I take someone with me. My best friend doesn't drink but likes going out, so she's the perfect DD. I never feel alone, and I always get home safe. She also keeps track of time so we don't get home *too* late.

Julie, Junior

I always eat a big meal and drink a bunch of water before I head to the club. It helps me avoid hangovers, and the bar food here is expensive.

Andre, Senior

Before I leave, I set a spending limit for the night and then only take that amount of money. Last year, I spent way too much on alcohol and had to ask my parents for money. It was a little embarrassing explaining what happened to the loans I had taken out. Now, I budget all my spending. Those loans have to last the whole semester.

Mark, Junior

I figure out how I'm getting home before I leave my house. Whether I'm walking, calling a cab, or finding a DD, I know what I'm doing before I head out the door. It makes life a lot easier when the night comes to a close.

Chris, Senior

My freshman year I went to a bunch of parties, but I never really talked to anybody. It took me a while, but I finally learned to get off my butt and talk to people. The party's not going to come to you.

Madison, Junior

My old roommate used to come in late from partying and pee all over everything. I guess he was seeing double and wanted to make sure to get urine into both toilets. I moved out the next semester. You want a good strategy for partying? How about don't pee on your roommate's stuff.

John, Junior

Throwing up at a party is one of the most humiliating things that can happen. Throwing up off a second floor balcony is even worse. Trust me, people don't let you forget that kind of thing. If you start to feel sick, go home. Don't sit around waiting for the lid to blow off.

Carrie, Senior

I don't drink, but a lot of my friends do, so I end up the designated driver a lot of the time. It's cool though because I get to demand my own terms. I never drive my own car. I never pay for gas. And I always get a free meal out of it. Being the only one who doesn't drink is actually pretty good. Plus, I get to sit back and watch my friends make complete fools of themselves.

Dave, Senior

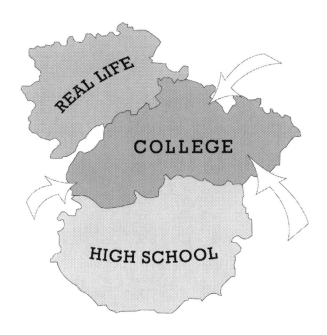

Sources

1 I obtained this info from the January 23, 2007 online article by "The Washington Post." The original source is the American Psychological Association. It can be found at: *http://www.washingtonpost.com/wp-dyn/content/ graphic/2007/01/22/GR2007012200620.html*.

2 CNNhealth has a ton of information. I found Dr. Sanjay Gupta's article on fat cells at: *http://www.cnn.com/ 2008/HEALTH/ dailydose/12/02/fat.cells/index.html*.

3 MensHealth.com is another wealth of information. This article is cleverly titled: "7 Reasons You're Still Hungry-Even After You Just Ate" and can be found at: *http://www.menshealth.com/mhlists/curb-hunger/*.

4 Bob Simon's heart wrenching article can be found at: *http://www.cbsnews.com/stories/2008/12/31/60minutes/main4694666.shtml*.

5 These facts and more can be found at *factsontap.org*. The site was founded to provide education and initiatives on alcohol and other drugs to high school and college students. If you have a question about alcohol, go there.

About the Author

Gabe Barrett grew up in Alexander City, Alabama before moving to Kentucky to finish out high school. He attended three universities during his five year college career. Gabe served as an RA, worked in the IT department, acted as president of a residential college, and even played football for Auburn University during that time. He graduated with a degree in English and is currently working on a number of books. He conquered college in 2010.

About the Artist

Jeff Lawrence also grew up in Alexander City, Alabama. He is currently studying Graphic Design at the University of Alabama. Jeff enjoys drawing fat birds and lightsaber duels, as well as surmounting impossible odds.